LIBRARY

This book is to be returned on or before the last date stamped below. Books recalled for another reader should be returned by the new date specified in the recall notice. Fines will be charged for books returned late.

UNIVERSITY COLLEGE CHESTER

A College of the
University of Liverpool

Short Loan

Coaches' Guide to Time Management

An official publication of the National Coaching Foundation

Coaches' Guide to Time Management

Charles Kozoll

SBL

Springfield Books Limited

© 1988 Charles Kozoll and the National Coaching Foundation

Published by Springfield Books Limited,
Norman Road, Denby Dale, Huddersfield HD8 8TH, West Yorkshire, England.

An official publication of the National Coaching Foundation, 4 College Close,
Beckett Park, Leeds LS6 3QH, West Yorkshire, England.

First edition 1988

Design: Douglas Martin
Illustrations: Bruce Baillie
Typesetting: Armitage Typo/Graphics Ltd, Huddersfield
Printed and bound in England by Biddles Limited, Guildford, Surrey

British Library Cataloguing in Publication Data
Kozoll, Charles
Coaches guide to time management.
1. Sports & games.   Coaching
I. Title   II. National Coaching Foundation
796'.07'7
ISBN 0-947655-32-8

Contents

Introduction

As a young college student stationed in East Africa years ago, I was introduced to "the Mixture." It was a unique remedy for an upset stomach, developed by a Scottish physician who had served many years in sub-Saharan Africa. Upon first treating me, this doctor prescribed a medicine to which he referred as *the* mixture, not *a* mixture. His irritable response to my inquiry about his choice of words was, "What you're getting, sonny, is *the* mixture that I've worked on for many years. It will take care of whatever ails you and can also be used to repair broken plates or patch holes in the screens around your house." The mixture did work on my stomach, although I never tried it out on plates or screens.

As a result, the word *the* signifying *one* way or *one* prescription has made me nervous ever since. My interest in time management has renewed this scepticism about single routes to solving often complex individual or group problems.

In preparing this book, I spoke to coaches in a variety of different sports and settings across the country. I examined these coaches' public statements and also collected many performers' comments about effective coaches. The results of this investigation have led me to suggest routes for effective time management for coaches. I offer no prescriptions, but suggest basic organising approaches which you can fit to your own coaching style, setting, and sport.

Coaches tend to be busy, energetic people, willing to accept many responsibilities. They are expected to manage complex training programmes and produce talented athletes in a highly pressured environment. Many coaches are volunteers who must juggle coaching with their careers and families. Frequently, they find themselves running frantically from task to task, trying to accomplish too much and very often accomplishing too little. Left with no time for themselves and for their friends and families, these coaches burn out mentally and physically.

Coaches' Guide to Time Management is for busy and overburdened coaches who want to control the pressure sports place on them. Time management is a means to an end, not an end in itself. The coaches who helped me develop this book emphasise that point. Effective time mangement will improve the quality of your life. As you read this book, carefully consider the contribution improved self-organisation could make to the success of your training programme, to the development of your athletes, and to the enjoyment you derive from coaching.

The book is divided into two parts. **Part 1** challenges you to examine your own time management effectiveness and also presents some examples of the problems experienced by coaches who manage time poorly. The basic elements of time management are explained, and coaches are encouraged to examine critically the organisation of their own coaching programmes. Organisational concerns common to all programmes are discussed and many suggestions offered for possible improvements.

Part 2 contains examples of time management techniques in practice. Case studies of full-time, part-time, and volunteer coaches illustrate different attitudes towards improving personal effectiveness. These coaches reveal highly personalised mangement systems which match their own unique personality characteristics. The book concludes with a review of recommended time management techniques and offers suggestions for developing and maintaining your own time management system.

Part One: Managing Time

Time is best managed when people understand why time is important and how it can easily be managed. **Part 1** of this book will explain both the 'why's' and the 'how's' of managing time.

Chapter 1 shows what happens when individuals and their organisations manage time poorly. The material comes, in part, from participants in time management seminars who reviewed their frantic days and saw how little they accomplished. In this chapter, you will meet two coaches who hurt themselves and others through their poor management of time. Although they operate very differently, these coaches prevent themselves from coaching effectively, making accomplishment difficult for both their athletes and assistants. The coaches are fictional, but their methods represent those of coaches I have interviewed and observed. The chapter concludes by introducing you to the ACORN environment, a chaotic environment which makes it difficult for people to reach their potential and work together as a cohesive, effective group.

In chapter 2 you are encouraged to analyse your own time use and evaluate your ACORN creating tendencies. Methods are presented for examining your effectiveness as a time manager and for identifying areas which would benefit from improved self-organisation.

Effective time management depends on the combination of two critical factors: direction and control. Chapter 3 outlines how to establish direction by setting realistic goals, priorities, and limits for your training programmes. Two key techniques for control are discussed in chapter 4: concentration and distress management. Maintaining control over coaching distractions and pressures will enable you to focus attention on improving the quality of your programme.

Successful and happy coaches who use time wisely have helped me prepare this book. The secret of their success is organisation. In conversations with coaches, I discovered many of them had unique systems which contributed to daily accomplishment and which kept pressure under control. In **Part 2,** you will meet some of these coaches and complete the development of your own personal recipe for effective time management.

Time management is an ongoing, continuous process, as is illustrated in the following chart. The steps in the chart correspond to chapters in this book. This chart will appear at the beginning of each chapter to remind you of the developmental cycle for improving your skills of time management.

1. Time management and sports

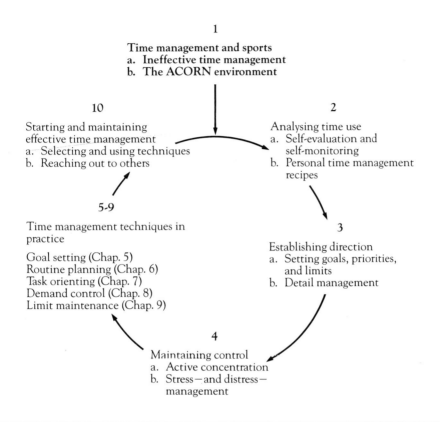

1

Time management and sports
a. Ineffective time management
b. The ACORN environment

10

Starting and maintaining
effective time management
a. Selecting and using techniques
b. Reaching out to others

2

Analysing time use
a. Self-evaluation and
self-monitoring
b. Personal time management
recipes

5-9

Time management techniques in
practice

Goal setting (Chap. 5)
Routine planning (Chap. 6)
Task orienting (Chap. 7)
Demand control (Chap. 8)
Limit maintenance (Chap. 9)

3

Establishing direction
a. Setting goals, priorities,
and limits
b. Detail management

4

Maintaining control
a. Active concentration
b. Stress — and distress —
management

Managing time

Everyone manages time — some well, some not so well. Poor time management has an adverse effect not only on the individual coach, but on all those who come into contact with the coach. Assistant coaches, physiotherapists, managers, performers, and others involved in the sport suffer the consequences of poor management in unpleasant and sometimes disastrous ways. Effective time management often means the difference between a successful and an unsuccessful training programme.

To illustrate this point, let us meet two coaches who manage their time poorly and see how they affect themselves and others. Effective time management is vital for both full-time and part-time or amateur coaches. In many ways, managing time is even more important for voluntary coaches who must juggle coaching responsibilities with a full-time job.

TWO POOR TIME MANAGERS

Sarah Steel and Frank Adams are both coaches working at a high level. Sarah is an office manager and a dedicated gymnastics coach. Frank is a full-time swimming coach employed by the local authority. Sarah spends her life on the run, always available and always willing to accept new responsibilities. In contrast Frank usually wanders around and procrastinates until he is under pressure. Then, with time running out, he frantically attemps to complete his work. The environments Sarah and Frank create are unpleasant both for themselves and for others. Working under these conditions stifles the potential of each coach, their assistants and performers. Let us examine in detail how Sarah and Frank manage (or mismanage) a typical week.

SARAH'S RACE AGAINST THE CLOCK

Sarah usually arrives at her office early, anticipating a busy day. Once she opens her door, it stays open all day except for three occasions: when she goes out for a lunchtime meeting, when she has a private talk with a colleague and when she leaves in the evening. Sarah is convinced she must always be accessible, regardless of her work load. The open door is a signal that others may interrupt her at any time.

During the morning, the open door invites passers-by to drop in for visits, to make requests, or to ask questions. Sarah never asks them to come back later, no matter how trivial the conversation. She is willing to talk or listen all morning and will even sometimes leave her office to chat to others in the corridor.

About mid-morning an assistant drops in to ask Sarah for help with a project: an inventory of office equipment is due by the end of the week. The assistant has been repeatedly instructed on how to do this task but does not enjoy counting and making lists. After listening to a few of the assistant's excuses, Sarah agrees to help. She clips the stack of inventory forms together and places them at the top of an already tall pile of papers sitting on her 'get to' table, which is the house for one tall stack of papers of theoretically high-priority activities. On another small desk and two tables, Sarah has piled forms, correspondence, announcements, and brochures. Sarah frequently wastes time looking for lost papers because she never sorts the important items from the unimportant ones.

THE PACE ACCELERATES

After the assistant leaves, Sarah tries to work, keeping her door open. The visits cease, but now the phone begins to ring. Two calls heighten Sarah's anxiety level. The first is from a friend who asks Sarah to arrange main speakers for next spring's coaching conference. Despite the likelihood of a hectic spring schedule, Sarah agrees to help her friend. The second call is from a company director who wants to know if Sarah has finished her work plan for the year. Controlling her panic, Sarah assures him that she is nearly done but chides herself, "Got to get on with that!"

At lunch time Sarah drives to a local school where she takes a school club. The preparation for this session is done en route to the school and in the relative calm of the journey she thinks of some excellent training ideas. She intends to write down her thoughts as soon as she arrives but gets caught up in various conversations and forgets them. After the session, several of the gymnasts thank Sarah for an excellent session. What Sarah does not hear as she hurries out is their whispered comments about her tense and pre-occupied appearance and whether or not they should continue inviting her to take the club.

NON-EXISTENT PLANNING

After eating a sandwich during the journey back from the school, Sarah returns to her office, determined to devote the afternoon to planning her work programme for the year. Although her diary is clear, Sarah has barely sat down at her desk when a troubled gymnast calls her on the telephone with a problem that cannot wait. Before Sarah can respond, the gymnast starts explaining the difficulty — one Sarah should have known about and taken steps to prevent. While the gymnast is explaining her problem, Sarah is worrying about her work plan. With her mind going in a dozen different directions at once, Sarah hears only about a third of what the gymnast is saying and this is evident in the inadequate response she gives to the gymnast's request for advice.

As the office closes, Sarah dashes home to plan the evening training session and get some tea. However, while she is preparing her tea, Sarah remembers another priority task—writing letters to two new gymnasts. If she does not do this soon, they will think she is not interested. Her paperwork at home is as disorganised as at work and it takes her ten minutes to find their letters; then she has to clear some space on her desk before she can get down to composing friendly replies. Halfway through the second paragraph, she remembers she forgot to complete the entry forms for the county championships. Sarah stops writing the letters and makes three long-distance calls to get forms. In fact, these were sent to her two weeks ago and are lying in one of the stacks on her crowded desk. In her panic Sarah does not stop to think whether or not she already has the forms; she only remembers this fact after £5 worth of long-distance calls and half an hour of nervous activity. On her way to the evening training session, she calls on an already overburdened club secretary with the blank forms and implores her to complete them. As she rushes out of the door she shouts the instructions: "Use the same information as last year! Need them by tomorrow! Thanks!" Sarah fails to notice the secretary's anger at having to bail her out again.

Sarah then rushes off to the training session with her club team which turns out to be a complete disaster. Gymnasts stand around with nothing to do and joke or just practice on their own. An assistant coach, if not continually coming up for directions, tries to improvise. Sarah, once a superior gymnast and a master technician, moves about the room giving hastily conceived instructions. At first, her lack of planning confuses the gymnasts and assistant coach, then later leaves them frustrated. Training ends with the gymnasts feeling dejected and ill-prepared and lacking confidence for the next competition.

When Sarah arrives home, the club secretary telephones to say, "Sarah, they have changed the entry forms for the county championships. The committee wants new information and you are the only one who has it." The secretary says she will return the forms to Sarah the next day and reminds her that they are already overdue and the club will have to pay a late entry fee. Sarah wonders how she is going to explain the late entry fee to the club treasurer.

Tuesday, Wednesday and Thursday's training sessions prove to be no better for Sarah. In fact as the week progresses, these days turn out to be even worse as Sarah grows increasingly more tense and frantic. Because Sarah is the leader of the club, her attitude is contagious. Coach and gymnasts snap at each other, culminating in poor performances at the club competition on Saturday.

FRANK'S TOO LEISURELY PACE

While Sarah represents one extreme of poor time management, Frank represents the other. On the surface, Frank appears calmer than Sarah, but he is equally disorganised. Frank is convinced that he does his best work under pressure. However, he does not understand how his assistant coach and swimmers feel about last minute efforts. Let us carefully look at one of Frank's typical weeks to see how he manages time.

A SLOW START

Frank shakes his head with a combination of awe and amusement as he watches colleagues run. That frantic pace is not for him. He prefers a more relaxed approach, at least at the beginning of the week. On Monday, he briefly reviews the last competition and decides what needs to be done at training. No immediate decision is taken, however, because Monday's and Tuesday's training sessions are always the same: the swimmers work on their own with a little guidance from the assistant coach. Frank wanders up and down the side of the pool watching.

Before training, Frank occupies himself with an assortment of interests and distractions. He skims articles, takes a long coffee break with friends, and works out for an hour before lunch. After lunch, he looks at some letters and forms but decides to put them aside until the next day. Frank does not notice that the secretary has underlined a deadline.

Before leaving for training, Frank reads through a new training equipment catalogue. "I'd never get the money for some of this stuff," he thinks. "The director would never agree." While daydreaming about the improvement this equipment would make to the swimmers' performance, the assistant coach interrupts him, wanting to discuss the next competition before training. "Let's leave it until tomorrow," Frank replies. His lack of interest is obvious, which discourages the assistant from making future suggestions.

The assistant coach is not the only one to notice Frank's apathy. Many of the swimmers wonder why Frank even bothers coming to training until Thursday when he finally begins to show concern. One enthusiastic administrator had to call three times to remind Frank about two exciting new young swimmers visiting this week's gala. Because Frank never returns the calls, the administrator himself makes arrangements for the visit but decides not to help out again because his efforts are not appreciated.

Early in the week, Frank always has time to drop in on the assistant coach to chat or to propose ideas and new work for him. These conversations end with, "Why don't you look into that?", leaving the assistant uncertain whether to treat the comment as a suggestion or as a firm request. Weekly team meetings have this same non-directive and indeterminate quality. Frank always seems more interested in proposing ideas than in dealing with the practical preparations for forthcoming events. He loathes details and considers such questions as what time the bus leaves trivial. Unfortunately, his assistants can't make certain decisions and Frank won't.

When he is calm and bored at the beginning of the week, Frank has a habit of interrupting others. He considers dropping in on colleagues a favour to them, thinking he is helping them to relax from their frenetic pace. Frank interrupts secretaries, facility managers, and administrators.

FIRST PROCRASTINATION, THEN PRESSURE

Frank follows the same relaxed pace on Tuesday and Wednesday, but early on Thursday morning his adrenalin begins to flow. Saturday is not so far away and the extent of what remains to be done suddenly dawns on him. On Thursday and Friday, Frank starts to resemble Sarah.

"Why didn't you tell me about that form?" he complains to the secretary after receiving a call about it. "Weren't you supposed to get me information on our opposition?" he asks the assistant coach. "You lot won't get anywhere with that attitude!" he yells to some swimmers who make mistakes when practising a new starting technique.

Thursday's and Friday's training sessions are active, intense and often confusing to swimmers. Although Frank is an able coach, he delivers his ideas too quickly, leaving the swimmers little time to absorb the suggestions. On Friday, Frank and his assistant coach try to catch up with last-minute details before the gala in vain. Luckily, it is a home gala, otherwise the swimmers would have had to make their own travel arrangements. At one away competition, the team did leave several bags of equipment behind because no one knew who was supposed to bring them.

In order to make the necessary arrangements, Frank has to plead for special favours "just one more time." Although he must do some photocopying outside the department and, therefore, at twice the cost, Frank only shrugs his shoulders. He has the same reaction upon learning what happened to the two new young swimmers. These young swimmers are given back row seats for the gala and a short tour of the facilities with the assistant coach. Frank does not bother to meet the young swimmers and they leave convinced they will not return. Frank's team wins on Saturday. Three key swimmers on the opposing team were injured the previous week and their replacements were much weaker, which compensated for Frank's poor preparation. "We didn't win, they lost," the assistant coach mumbles. Meanwhile, Frank congratulates the swimmers, adding that they do their best work under pressure. Although Frank notices the changing room is strangely silent after his last comment, he considers this only momentarily and leaves.

POOR TIME MANAGEMENT

Let us review Frank's management of the weekly coaching schedule. The week begins at a too leisurely pace, then finishes with frantic last minute preparation. Because Frank believes he works better under pressure, he does not notice a problem with his time management. In contrast, Sarah believes she cannot change her frantic days to more controlled ones. Her door is open and cannot be closed. She feels obligated to take on more and reacts to events on a day-to-day basis instead of being guided by a plan of action. Tragically, the potential of both coaches remains unrealised because of their poor time management. In addition, their actions create environments which gymnasts, swimmers, assistants and supporters find stressful and unpleasant. These elements can be simply summarised with one acronym: ACORN.

The ACORN setting

ACORN is an acronym describing the environment Sarah and Frank create for the people around them. Those who must work in this setting—coaches, assistant coaches, swimmers, gymnasts, secretaries, administrators and many others, gradually become Aggressive, Compulsive, Ornery and, finally, Really Nutty.

THE EFFECTS OF POOR TIME MANAGEMENT

If we look closer at Sarah's Monday, we can see just how many people she harmed by her poor time management.

1. The friend who asked Sarah to find a speaker, for it is doubtful Sarah will successfully accomplish this.
2. The director whose concern over her work plan was left unresolved.
3. The two prospective gymnasts who are left to wonder if Sarah is interested in them. They probably will not show any further interest in attending Sarah's sessions.
4. The school club members who notice Sarah's tenseness and begin to wonder if she can handle the job.
5. The organisers of the national championship who will probably receive incorrectly filled-out forms.
6. The overworked secretary who was asked to do another last minute salvaging job—something she will be increasingly less willing to do in the future.
7. The gymnast who looked to Sarah for help, yet barely received a third of Sarah's attention—a fact the gymnast may have mentioned to other teammates.
8. The entire team of potentially successful gymnasts and assistant coach, who are frustrated by a lack of direction.
9. Everyone else whose life Sarah has made harder through her ineffectiveness. Eventually, her methods will create such bad feelings that she will not find any support when she most needs it.

Frank has a similar effect on others including:

1. The secretary who is criticised for not pointing out the deadline—something she did do earlier in the week.
2. The enthusiastic assistant who wanted to share information about the team's next opponents and was turned away.
3. The swimmers who are frustrated by Frank's lack of concern early in the week and by his unrealistic expectations at the last minute.
4. The administrator who wanted to help but whose efforts were ignored—he won't help again.
5. The assistant coach who is never certain what action to take following Frank's proposals and who is frustrated by Frank's inability to make decisions.
6. Others in the department whose work Frank interrupts whenever he feels bored.

Frank deceives himself by believing he does his best work under pressure. Sometimes he is lucky, and his swimmers still win. But with or without luck, Frank frustrates everyone in contact with him. Procrastinating early in the week wastes valuable thinking and planning time. Frank lets his own time evaporate and he interrupts others who are trying to do their own jobs.

On Thursdays and Fridays, when he and his team must cram a week's worth of preparation into two frantic days, Frank makes mistakes and forgets important details. Although Frank claims to work best under pressure, he begins blaming others for what they were unable to do because of his procrastination.

Sarah's and Frank's assistants and gymnasts/swimmers want to contribute to the team's success, and all have valuable contributions to make. Unfortunately, Frank and Sarah do not make use of the information, talent, and advice available. The lack of sensitivity erodes the loyalty and support of others. In short, Sarah and Frank make life miserable for other people; they create ACORN environments and fail to consider how their actions affect others. They do not realise that time is a collective resource which must be used intelligently for the benefit of all, not something for their personal use only.

TIME AS A COLLECTIVE RESOURCE

Time management techniques are often prescribed to help individuals improve themselves. But individual improvement is often dependent on the cooperation of others. Efforts to improve time management may fail without the understanding and endorsement of your family and colleagues. Coaches often find themselves in situations where they suffer the effects of other coaches' disorganisation. The disorganised behaviour of Sarah and Frank affected many people negatively, creating a chaotic and aimless working environment. If you, too, are a poor time manager, you are probably reducing the productivity and success of others around you.

Coaches manage environments. Regardless of the sport or whether you are coaching 'novices' or team members, you are responsible for creating and maintaining a healthy working environment. This includes a well-planned programme with a clear sense of direction, realistic limits, and a climate that encourages individual and group productivity. In other words, you must strive to create an atmosphere in which people enjoy working together.

Before continuing to discuss how you can ensure that your training programme has direction, limits, and a calm but productive climate, let's examine the management problems contributing to an ACORN environment.

Management problems contributing to an ACORN environment

Research has indicated that poor time managers generally suffer from one or more of the following management problems:

- Relying on 'mythical time'
- Underestimating demands on time
- Task creep
- Task hopping
- Ignoring reality

In the next section we examine each of these management problems in more detail. You will then be able to re-examine your own management skills and avoid the mistakes Sarah and Frank made.

RELYING ON 'MYTHICAL TIME'

This management problem leads to putting off assignments in the mistaken belief you will later have a larger block of uninterrupted time available in which to complete your assignments. Sarah believed she would have the afternoon to do her work programme. Her reliance on free time that did not exist — mythical time — lulled her into thinking she had plenty of time. Consequently, she allowed herself to be overly accessible in the morning. The 'real' time she had on Monday morning could have been valuably used. It is easy to believe that you will have more time in the future than you do at present. Unfortunately, when the future arrives, you quickly discover that this belief was indeed a myth.

By relying on mythical time, Sarah gave away her real time. In the afternoon her free time was eaten away by legitimate demands: a gymnast with a problem and enquiries that urgently needed to be answered. Sarah knows her mornings will be frequently interrupted by visitors and telephone calls and encourages these interruptions by keeping her door open. Sarah does not recognise that she will always have interruptions, both in the morning and in the afternoon. Instead of leaving large, important tasks for later, she should start taking care of them immediately. She could divide complex, high-priority tasks into smaller, more manageable pieces. She could make one major activity — such as planning her work programme — the morning's single focus. With this approach, Sarah would depend less on mythical time and give priorities the immediate attention they deserve.

In a similar way, Frank put off any form of planning or organisation until the end of the week. He failed to recognise that it was impossible to complete team preparations successfully in the time he made available. He avoided high-priority tasks early in the week instead of giving them immediate attention. The week ended in panic, creating a stressful situation for swimmers, coaches and others associated with Frank's work.

UNDERESTIMATING DEMANDS ON TIME

As an office manager and a coach, Sarah must respond to the legitimate demands others make on her time, accounting for a large part of her day. Sarah could accomplish more if she recognised how much time she actually controlled as well as how much she cannot control. If we consider the time she devotes to coaching we can see that she needs to use her time carefully. Tasks such as planning training sessions and filling out entry forms must be given high priority. Time will also need to be allocated for gymnasts needing to discuss problems (preferably out of working hours!), parents wishing to discuss their child's performance or other coaches needing an impromptu meeting to discuss new ideas or to resolve problems. Finally, there will always be unexpected crises to cope with, such as tracking down missing equipment, taking care of an injured gymnast, holding an emergency committee meeting or finding new accommodation when the old facilities are lost.

Sarah treats many of these tasks as intrusions into her ideally uncluttered, mythical time. However, they are an integral part of coaching and Sarah should make time to deal with them.

Setting priorities is a key element in the effective use of time. Encouraging new gymnasts and planning for training are priority activities and should receive priority attention. Discussing a problem with a gymnast should receive complete rather than half-hearted attention. No matter how effective Sarah's planning and organisation she must learn to live with the unexpected. If Sarah recognised this she would realistically evaluate her ability to accept new tasks.

TASK CREEP

Task creep is the problem of failing to complete immediate tasks before agreeing to do more. If Sarah stayed within the time she controls each day, she would carry a lighter load of truly essential activities and could integrate legitimate requests and crises more easily. Unfortunately, because Sarah does not recognise how little time she actually has, she fills her schedule with too many non-essential tasks. As Sarah continues to accept more and more tasks, she forgets what she already has to do: Sarah agrees to help with an inventory that is her assistant's responsibility; she agrees to find a speaker for next year's national conference; and she agrees to finish the work plan immediately, without requesting any assistance.

The results of task creep are obvious: (a) Sarah is forced to lie to the company director; (b) she wastes time (hers and the secretary's) and money on the national championship forms; (c) she gives an ill-prepared session to the school club; (d) she listens half-heartedly to a troubled gymnast; and (e) she holds haphazard, discouraging training sessions.

Controlling task creep requires more frequent use of the word NO. Many people find this is a hard word to use. But hard is not impossible, and lightening the load will do much to eliminate an ACORN environment.

TASK HOPPING

Task hopping is the result of poor concentration. This is caused by too many tasks and too little sense of priority. Task hopping coaches are easily identified: they stare into space; they look around and are always searching to find a form or a manual; they wait in anticipation of a telephone call or a visit; and they listen to others or perform one task while thinking about others.

Both Sarah and Frank are task hoppers. Frank flips through some important forms, then puts them down to skim practice plans. He develops then drops ideas and does not complete anything. Sarah starts one task, interrupting it to start another. She thinks up good ideas but loses them because she does not write them down. Both Frank and Sarah task hop by creating unnecessary interruptions—Sarah by being too accessible and Frank by procrastinating.

IGNORING REALITY

Ignoring reality is perhaps the hardest problem to correct because you must examine yourself with a critical and objective eye. Ignoring reality is ignoring the fact that certain personal traits and beliefs undermine rather than enhance a work programme. Sarah ignores reality by clinging to the belief that she must always be accessible. Her accessibility and unrealistic willingness to serve prevent her from attending to important work.

Frank's belief that he works best under pressure means that he spends three days bothering everyone else and two panicky days making errors, forgetting important details, and blaming others for his poor preparation. Ignoring reality also means ignoring the effects of these personal traits on others. Sarah and Frank are responsible for overburdening already swamped assistants, letting down friends and supporters, and hurting others' feelings.

Summary and recommendations

The coaches described in this chapter experienced problems familiar to all poor time managers. Sarah Steel attempted too much and in trying to meet all her responsibilities failed to attend to the most important tasks. Frank Adams confused and frustrated his swimmers and assistants because of his insensitivity and his tendency to avoid responsibilities until the last minute. Both coaches suffered because of a lack of planning and self-organisation. These managerial behaviours are frequently the source of organisational problems. The potential of the two coaches, their assistants, and their teams was not realised. Effective time management is critical to the success of all coaching programmes. Therefore, as a coach you should recognise the following:

1. Time is a collective resource. Coaches' management of environments affects how others manage time and influences the achievement of individual and programme success.
2. By mismanaging your own time, you create stressful working environments for your colleagues.
3. You may create ACORN environments: climates in which people become Aggressive, Compulsive, Ornery and Really Nutty.
4. Five management problems contribute to the development of an ACORN environment. These include (a) relying on mythical time, (b) underestimating demands on time, (c) task creep, (d) task hopping, and (e) ignoring reality.

Coaches with poor management skills can have a disastrous effect on a coaching programme. The next chapter will take a closer look at time and will examine your effectiveness as a time manager.

2. Analysing time use

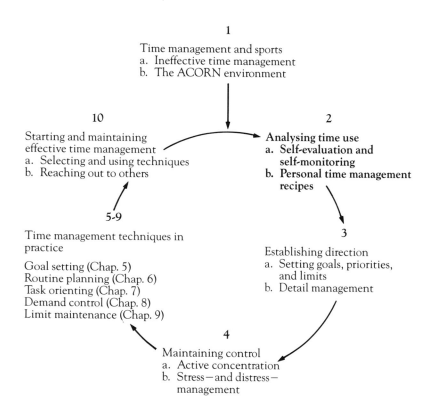

1

Time management and sports
a. Ineffective time management
b. The ACORN environment

10

Starting and maintaining
effective time management
a. Selecting and using techniques
b. Reaching out to others

2

Analysing time use
a. **Self-evaluation and**
   self-monitoring
b. **Personal time management**
   recipes

5-9

Time management techniques in
practice

Goal setting (Chap. 5)
Routine planning (Chap. 6)
Task orienting (Chap. 7)
Demand control (Chap. 8)
Limit maintenance (Chap. 9)

3

Establishing direction
a. Setting goals, priorities,
   and limits
b. Detail management

4

Maintaining control
a. Active concentration
b. Stress—and distress—
   management

Self-evaluating

The last chapter described some of the problems created by poor time management. Sarah Steel and Frank Adams did not appreciate the impact their ineffective time management had on others. Neither recognised the problems caused by their poor organisation, believing that these problems were beyond their control. To be an effective time manager, you must first understand the extent to which outcomes are dependent on your organisational skills. Failing to accept this responsibility inevitably creates management problems.

The battered mind, or where am I going now?

Mzungu is the Kiswahili word for anyone with a white skin. The East Africans who coined the word say it describes individuals who wander around with no apparent direction. Legend has it that Africans watched European explorers criss-cross the countryside and 'discover' lakes and mountains the Africans had known about for centuries.

The same lack of direction is common in many environments. Sarah was definitely mzungu on Monday as she jumped from task to task. By Thursday mzungu behaviour had spread to Frank who now faced too many tasks in the time available. Mzungu behaviour is displayed by many coaches who attempt too much or fail to control their environment. Eventually, these mzungus begin to feel mentally battered and accomplish little.

'The battered mind' describes a condition experienced by managers in business, industry and government. These individuals spend' their days running from one activity to another, never taking any time to think or to plan. Mentally and physically exhausted each evening, they return home unable to enjoy time with family and friends. Gradually, their energy is depleted and burnout sets in. Coaches often recognise the symptoms of the battered mind but unfortunately are convinced they must live with this state of mind until exhaustion forces them out of the sport. The mind is not equipped for that kind of consistent beating: the result is a dangerous form of helplessness which can easily affect others in the working environment. Coaches who have a battered mind are often the instigators of ACORN environments.

Coaches who realise that their minds are being battered admit to having some of these problems. Because they do not determine their priorities, they task hop, allow their minds to wander and digress, anticipate interruptions and bounce up and down instead of attending to essential tasks. Rather than giving sustained attention to the truly important work, these coaches make constant interruption a tradition. Coaches will frequently swear that they do their best work under pressure. For some coaches, it seems that an approaching deadline is the only way to motivate interest and stimulate real effort.

Coaches who admit to the battered mind note the rapid pace of life and the insufficient time they have to accomplish all their responsibilities. These coaches, who should be in control of their environment, are slaves to a multitude of external forces they believe are beyond their control. They work longer and longer hours and still there is more to do!

In the last chapter Sarah Steel, Frank Adams and others suffered a number of unpleasant experiences because of poor time management. These poor time managers created ACORN environments in which people moved from crisis to crisis. The coaches became tense and exhausted; they accomplished less and even this was done poorly.

Five management problems were identified which contribute to the development of an ACORN environment—a situation in which people become Aggressive, Compulsive, Ornery and Really Nutty. As you read the chapter you probably began wondering about the effectiveness of your own time management skills. You may already be aware of some problem areas, but it is difficult to evaluate yourself objectively. To help you evaluate your ACORN tendencies, you should respond honestly to the questions listed in the ACORN Self-Evaluation questionnaire (overleaf).

What was your score? If your total was forty or above, beware of ACORN-related problems. A total between thirty and forty is cause for concern. Regardless of where you scored, avoid complacency. Even the best time managers can slip. It is a good idea to check your answers with colleagues, for you may discover they perceive your behaviour differently.

This simple self-evaluation may have revealed time management problems you had not previously noticed. Unfortunately, the self-evaluation does suffer from the limitation that it relies on your perceptions of reality. It is possibly you failed to observe other problems that exist. To help you identify specific problems, a useful technique is to self-monitor.

ACORN SELF-EVALUATION

Use this questionnaire to assess your ACORN-creating potential. All of us are prone to create environments similar to those of Sarah and Frank. By checking these questions once or twice a week, we can monitor our behaviour and improve our time management. Circle the number which most accurately represents your honest response to the statement.

1. I rely on mythical time, putting off major work until 'later'.

1	2	3	4	5
Rarely		Sometimes		Often

2. I overestimate the amount of time I control each day.

1	2	3	4	5
Rarely		Sometimes		Often

3. I readily accept new tasks and am reluctant to say no to a request.

1	2	3	4	5
Rarely		Sometimes		Often

4. My days are spent hopping from one task to another because concentrating is difficult where I work.

1	2	3	4	5
Rarely		Sometimes		Often

5. My door stays open as an invitation to drop-in visitors.

1	2	3	4	5
Rarely		Sometimes		Often

6. I will put aside my work if a colleague requests assistance.

1	2	3	4	5
Rarely		Sometimes		Often

7. I change priorities if a new task or idea interests me.

1	2	3	4	5
Rarely		Sometimes		Often

8. My best work is done under deadline pressure and I usually finish just in time.

1	2	3	4	5
Rarely		Sometimes		Often

9. I am insensitive to others' need for privacy to accomplish their work.

1	2	3	4	5
Rarely		Sometimes		Often

10. Those with whom I work feel pressured because of my tendencies to procrastinate.

1	2	3	4	5
Rarely		Sometimes		Often

Self-monitoring

Self-monitoring involves collecting detailed data on what happens each day. Many consultants on executive effectiveness suggest that time be recorded in fifteen or thirty minute intervals. An alternative and less time-consuming monitoring technique is to set aside two ten-minute periods, one before lunch and the other before leaving in the afternoon, to review what you have done that day. Shown below is the format for a time chart on which you can record your daily activities.

Date: _____ Name: _____		Date: _____ Name: _____	
Time	**Activity**	**Time**	**Activity**
6.00 am		3.00	
6.30		3.30	
7.00		4.00	
7.30		4.30	
8.00		5.00	
8.30		5.30	
9.00		6.00	
9.30		6.30	
10.00		7.00	
10.30		7.30	
11.00		8.00	
11.30		8.30	
12.00		9.00	
12.30 pm		9.30	
1.00		10.00	
1.30		10.30	
2.00		11.00	
2.30		11.30	

With self-monitoring, data replace conjecture. Our memories are so fragile that it is easy to forget what we plan to do, as well as what we have done. With periodic self-monitoring, you can take snapshots of your busy life. The time chart above can be used to analyse specific days that may be more important than others: for example, the days leading up to a major game or competition, the period immediately after it, or the time spent on a coaching course. The data you gather will make it easier to pinpoint ACORN-producing activities.

In private organisations, senior managers will often ask talented but disorganised employees to monitor their daily activities. After a week, these employees are generally shocked by what they observe. They become alert to where task creep begins and how easily a new option or interruption can throw them off track. These individuals continue by reviewing typical days at least three times a month. This enables them to pick up any backsliding and helps them catch the reappearance of bad habits. Many people elect to self-monitor more often, sometimes on specific days or for short periods on especially hectic days. The habit of self-monitoring is a way of keeping unproductive time-use practices from reappearing.

By completing the daily time chart, you will be taking an essential first step in time management. You must know how to spend your time before you can plan how to use it more effectively. "But isn't keeping this log just an additional waste of time?" is a frequent question to the idea of a time chart. My response is to suggest they at least try the exercise, then evaluate its worth. Research has shown that most people are very inaccurate in assessing the time they spend on daily activities. For many, it is a revelation to discover they spend two or three hours a day on the phone or only fifteen minutes a day on priority tasks. You will be able to determine objective standards by which to evaluate the effectiveness of your daily organisation only after you know where your time goes.

Monitoring would be a valuable exercise to recommend to coaches like Sarah and Frank. The evidence of real data can lead to genuine improvement. To illustrate, we will examine how Sarah Steel might have completed the time chart on the day we observed her behaviour.

If Sarah looked at the chart carefully, she would begin to notice how her day was filled with constant interruptions and how little time she actually spent working toward her goals.

Date: MAY 8th　　　Name: SARAH STEEL	
Time	**Activity**
6.00 am	
6.30	
7.00	WOKE, SHOWERED
	DRESSED
7.30	BREAKFAST
	DROVE TO OFFICE
8.00	ARRIVED AT THE OFFICE
	CHECKED YESTERDAY'S POST
8.30	CHATTED WITH SECRETARY & OTHER STAFF - OFFICE CLEANER
	CALLED- WON'T BE IN TODAY, ARRANGED SUBSTITUTE
9.00	WORKED ON WORK PROGRAMME
	TWO COLLEAGUES VISIT
9.30	DISCUSSED WITH BILL AND WENDY APPOINT. OF NEW
	STAFF
10.00	DISCUSSED INVENTORY REPORT WITH JOAN- OFFERED
	TO HELP. SHE CALLED- I'LL GET NATIONAL CONFERENCE SPEAKERS
10.30	COFFEE BREAK
	READ SPORTS JOURNALS
11.00	DIRECTOR CALLED- WORK PLAN NEEDED IMMEDIATELY
11.30	DEALING WITH DAILY CORRESPONDENCE
12.00	DROVE TO SCHOOL
12.30 pm	SCHOOL GYMNASTICS CLUB
1.00	DRIVE BACK TO OFFICE
1.30	BEGAN WRITING WORK PLAN
2.00	J. W. TELEPHONED (PERSONAL PROBLEM)
2.30 - 4.30	INTERVIEWS FOR NEW STAFF ALL AFTERNOON

Date: MAY 8th　　　Name: SARAH STEEL	
Time	**Activity**
3.00	
3.30	
	INTERVIEWS
4.00	
4.30	
5.00	DROVE HOME FROM WORK
	SHOPPING
5.30	PREPARED TEA AND ATE
6.00	BEGAN LETTERS TO TWO NEW PLAYERS (10 mins)
	LOOKED FOR COUNTY CHAMPIONSHIP ENTRY FORMS
6.30	DROVE TO CLUB SECRETARY'S HOUSE & LEFT FORMS
7.00	ARRIVED AT TRAINING
	EQUIPMENT OUT AND CHECKED
7.30	TRAINING
	ASSISTANT COACH SEEMS DOWN- MUST TALK TO HER
8.00	TRAINING. - GYMNAST WITH AN INJURY - MUST
	CONTACT PHYSIOTHERAPIST
8.30	TRAINING. - TRANSPORT PROBLEMS FOR NEXT MONTH'S
	CHAMPIONSHIPS- MUST CHECK WITH BUS COMPANY
9.00	DRIVE HOME
9.30	TELEPHONE CALL FROM CLUB SECRETARY ABOUT
	CHAMPIONSHIP ENTRY FORMS
10.00	WATCHED T. V. WHILE IRONING CLOTHES
10.30	WATCHED REST OF T.V. SHOW
11.00	GOT READY FOR BED
	SLEPT
11.30	

A clearer analysis of this data can be seen if we divide it under headings representing the major activities in Sarah's daily schedule. Table 2.1 illustrates this next step.

The Time Chart Analysis clearly shows how inefficiently Sarah used her time on this particular day. She spent 60 minutes in unplanned meetings, was continually interrupted throughout the day for a total of one hour, and wasted one hour of her time on self-imposed interruptions.

From this analysis it is easy to see how much time Sarah wastes each day on non-essential tasks, and how little time she devotes to her major responsibilities. Looking at these figures might help Sarah understand why she never seems able to catch up or finish her tasks. However, analysing only one day might give a distorted impression of her time use. Sarah ought to keep a Time Chart for a week. Everyone occasionally experiences exceptional days of unexpected distractions resulting in lost time. Over a week the exceptions become less noticeable, and a regular

TABLE 2.1
TIME CHART ANALYSIS

Activities	Hours
Personal	
Sleep 11 p.m. – 7 a.m.	8
Shower/dress	¼
Breakfast	¼
Lunch (coaching session)	1
Tea	½
Shopping	¼
Ironing	½
	10¾
Travel	
To office	¼
Return home	¼
To and from lunch	¼
To and from training session	½
	1¼
Work	
Routine calls/post	1
Meetings (unplanned)	1
(planned)	1
Interruptions (by others)	1
(self-imposed)	1
Interviews	2
Work programme	½
	7½
Coaching	
Administration	½
Training session	2
Club secretary (¼hr, ¼hr)	½
	3
Leisure	
Watching T.V.	1
Reading sports journal	½
	1½

pattern of time-use emerges. The following are some of the insights Sarah would gain:

—   An average two hours a day is spent in conversation.
—   Planning for training takes place en route to sessions.
—   Interruptions are a continual problem.
—   Poor organisation of paperwork causes much waste of time.

Through self-monitoring, time management problems become more apparent. Until coaches understand that they are experiencing management problems, it is futile to suggest possible remedies. If coaches like Sarah and Frank can be encouraged to monitor themselves, they will begin to recognise the need for improvement. They may also begin to appreciate the stressful environments they create for colleagues, as well as the limitations their behaviour places on the eventual success of the training programme. Many of the problems the two coaches faced were discussed in detail in chapter 1. To resolve these organisational problems, the best approach is to try to improve your time management skills rather than dwell on the negative. This will help prevent the emergence of the original difficulties. Sarah and Frank would benefit from this approach, and it will also work for you.

Before continuing to learn about techniques for improving your management of time, it is essential to become aware of your existing behaviour. You need to collect objective data and analyse how effectively you currently manage time. Even if you feel you are already an effective time manager, you will benefit most from this book by conducting an objective examination. Use the time charts previously presented and through careful analysis, try to identify a few areas in which you feel there is some room for improvement.

Once you understand the pattern of your own time use, the next step towards becoming a good time manager is to identify the techniques you already use to manage time. At the end of each day for a one- to two-week period, spend five to ten minutes reviewing your accomplishments. Try to identify which organising techniques you regularly or periodically use. For example, do you have a daily schedule? Do you set aside periods of time to complete tasks? Do you have a system for dealing with routine paperwork? Some of you may discover you already have a system which works. If so, reading this book will reinforce your experiences and boost your self-confidence. Additional techniques to improve your time management will be suggested throughout this book. These will reduce your ACORN-causing tendencies and will increase your productivity.

For the moment, however, let us begin by emphasising what already works and build on existing foundations. List on two reminder cards the useful techniques you already use. To remind yourself of them, leave one card in your office and another at home. Put the cards in visible locations—for example, above your telephone or on your clipboard. You may also want to carry a copy with you as a constant reference whenever you feel a need for direction. This is the reverse of the 'out of sight, out of mind' principle; it increases the probability that you will use the techniques you have chosen.

For the first week or two, review these lists at the end of each day. What did you achieve? Focus on your successes—for example, a well-planned practice, a routine task completed, or a major competition arranged. Carefully evaluate the extent to which your existing time management techniques contributed to these successes. The steps for constructing your own personal method for successful time management are listed below:

— Write down techniques which already work on reminder index cards.
— Post them in visible locations.
— Review them as a habitual part of your daily routine.
— Relate accomplishments to the regular use of your techniques.

As you continue reading this book, keep some index cards nearby and note down any ideas that appeal to you. It is unrealistic to expect to become an effective time manager overnight. This ability is developed slowly by experimenting with a variety of organising methods and by discovering what works best for you. Your goal is to construct a personal recipe for successful time management. We will return to this list and its use in the introduction to **Part 2** and again in chapter 10. By then, you will have had the chance to modify or adapt your ideas based on the advice given in the following chapters.

Summary and recommendations

To become effective time managers, coaches must first understand the extent to which the success of their programmes is dependent on their organisational skills. Listed below are things to consider when analysing your ability to manage time:

1. If you attempt too much or fail to control the pressures in your environment, you will not realise your coaching potential and will frustrate the efforts of others in your sport.
2. Remain alert to behaviour which creates ACORN environments.
3. Self-evaluation and self-monitoring are two methods for identifying time management problems.
4. Analysing the data collected on a daily time chart provides objective evidence of your effectiveness as a time manager.
5. Recognising areas where there is room for improving your time use will give you the motivation to attempt remedial action.
6. List the organising techniques you already use on reminder cards, and relate your accomplishments to the effectiveness of these techniques.

Once you understand the effectiveness of your own time management skills, you can begin to consider methods for improvement. You must build on the basis of your existing organisational skills. The next chapter will examine the necessity of establishing a clear direction as you organise your programme.

3. Establishing direction

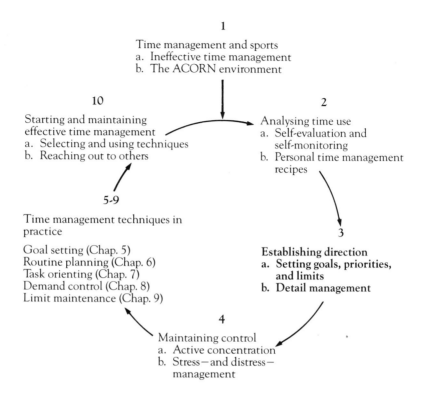

1

Time management and sports
a. Ineffective time management
b. The ACORN environment

10

Starting and maintaining
effective time management
a. Selecting and using techniques
b. Reaching out to others

2

Analysing time use
a. Self-evaluation and
   self-monitoring
b. Personal time management
   recipes

5-9

Time management techniques in
practice

Goal setting (Chap. 5)
Routine planning (Chap. 6)
Task orienting (Chap. 7)
Demand control (Chap. 8)
Limit maintenance (Chap. 9)

3

Establishing direction
a. Setting goals, priorities,
and limits
b. Detail management

4

Maintaining control
a. Active concentration
b. Stress—and distress—
   management

Goal setting

Good time management is not an end in itself but rather a means to an
end. It can make you personally more efficient and create a pleasant and
productive working environment for your colleagues. But to be successful,
you must clearly identify the ends you are seeking. You need direction.
The first step in developing effective time management skills is to define
clearly your goals. Goals give you a basis for setting priorities, making
decisions and working for some things while eliminating others. Realistic
goals and a sense of direction will prevent the creation of an ACORN
environment.

"Which path shall I take?" Alice asked the March Hare when she came
to a crossroads. "Where do you want to go?" the Hare responded. "I don't
know!" Alice admitted. "Then the choice isn't important", replied the
Hare.

The Hare's message is clear and valid: proceeding without a sense of direction and specific goals is often a waste of time and energy. Goals provide the foundation for a successful training programme. Many kinds of goals can be set: lifetime, five-year, one-year, seasonal. The choice is yours, but it is essential you identify a clear sense of immediate direction.

Your goals will depend on your coaching philosophy. The philosophy conceived by Rainer Martens and endorsed by the National Coaching Foundation is *Athletes First, Winning Second.* This philosophy emphasises that your first goal is to help all your performers fully develop their physical, emotional, mental and social abilities. Performers who understand you are primarily concerned with their development and their striving for success will enjoy participating in your training regardless of results. Removing the fear of failure helps them to perform better and, in the long term, achieve greater success.

It is unrealistic to evaluate the success of your training programme solely on the basis of your win-loss record. In sport, not every team can win, and many factors other than individual or team performance contribute to the final game result. It is important to instil in your performers the understanding that winning or losing should not be the measure of their success. In trying to plan a successful, beneficial and enjoyable training programme, you must first be *realistic.*

SETTING REALISTIC GOALS

Ideally, you should identify realistic goals before the season begins. These must include your coaching goals *and* quality of life goals which include activities with family and friends and time for relaxation, hobbies, self-improvement, and perhaps some community obligations. Success-driven coaches easily forget these essential activities. If you fail to set limits on what you will attempt, you will eliminate personal time for activities other than coaching. Sarah is an example of this type of coach. Because of her willingness to try to do everything, she failed to complete anything successfully. For a busy coach, a more effective approach is to do less, better, *and* to find time to stop.

"I don't have time to relax, let alone develop a hobby," busy and often overcommitted individuals will exclaim. These individuals describe all their responsibilities, their committees, meetings, reports, special projects and extra work. Because they could not say no, they created a packed schedule with no time left for rest and fun. These individuals soon wear out and, in the long run, will never feel successful.

A realistic blend of professional and personal goals should be the motivation for managing time. You must clearly identify your goals and share them with colleagues, athletes and family members. Write your programme goals and give everyone associated with the programme a copy. This sense of direction will help you stay in control of your day. Without control, it is difficult and often impossible to accomplish any goals.

THE PROCESS OF ESTABLISHING GENERAL GOALS

To give you some idea of this goal-setting process, you should begin by choosing general goals for your career (which may or may not be full-time coaching), family, personal development and community service. For example, Sarah Steel might establish the following general goals:

Coaching Goal   To be an effective coach and to help all my gymnasts fully develop their physical, emotional, mental and social abilities.

Family   To live in the country but near large town amenities, earning a salary which will enable me to buy my own home. To marry and raise a small family.

Personal Development   To keep fit, to learn how to prepare vegetarian meals, to improve my guitar playing and to learn French so I can visit Paris during the summer holidays.

Community Service   To continue offering coaching clinics for young gymnasts during the holidays, and actively to support other community events (but to avoid overcommitting myself).

General goals tend to be vague statements of future directions you would like to follow. They provide a basis for identifying more specific goals which will lead to the adoption of certain patterns of behaviour. For example, Sarah's general coaching goal demands attention to the creation of a well-organised coaching programme. Before Sarah can begin planning the steps necessary to achieve this goal, she must decide whether the goal is one of her priorities. By selecting this goal, she may have to postpone, temporarily or permanently, the realisation of other general goals.

Setting priorities

It is not realistic to set goals, or to expect to achieve them, without first deciding priorities. Your priorities are your street signs; without them, you can wander down any number of side streets and never reach your destination.

To change metaphors, imagine your priorities as a set of three concentric circles. The inner ring in this picture contains the work that only you can do—these are your highest priority tasks. As events occur, ask yourself if they fit into this inner ring. Remember that some routine chores have priority; for example, the competition entry forms that Sarah and Frank neglected to complete were in this ring.

The maintenance of your programme is a high priority. Shown below is a list of highest priority tasks gleaned from conversations with successful coaches. As your coaching programme grows and matures, you can add new challenges or variations to this inner ring. But, as several coaches have advised, "Do the tricky stuff once the basics are in place!"

PROGRAMME MAINTENANCE ACTIVITIES

— Planning practices
— Monitoring individual and team performances
— Planning for competitions
— Necessary paperwork
— Time for athletes to discuss problems

PROGRAMME BUILDING ACTIVITIES

— Providing information to committee members
— General public relations
— Talent identification and selection
— Programme monitoring
— Facilities and equipment review

In addition to the tasks you have labelled 'highest priority,' you may want to consider a second ring of 'maybe' tasks. You may get to one of these assignments or activities, if there is time, but only after the highest priority tasks are finished or under control. Remember, Murphy's Law states that everything takes longer than expected. Do not be like Sarah who trapped herself in the low-priority tasks of the second and third ring groups of activities.

This third ring contains 'never do' activities. These might include agreeing to referee a game, volunteering to help another coach, or taking on more committee responsibilities. Although they may be pleasant and even helpful services, avoid these tasks, for tasks in the third ring take precious time away from those essential tasks in the inner ring.

Coaching, either on a full-time or part-time basis, is a time-consuming job. It is easy for busy and committed coaches to forget the time they need for themselves and for loved ones. This personal time also belongs in the inner ring. Just like a savings account, you must set aside a little time each day, or you may find too late that you have nothing at all. For example, from her list of general goals, Sarah Steel ought to identify activities other than those related to coaching for inclusion in her list of high priorities. She might include some of the following:

— Taking a daily midday break to run or exercise
— Attending a guitar class two evenings a week
— Leaving work no later than 6 p.m. every day and becoming more socially active
— Visiting her parents at least once a week

Another coach might include the following list of personal activities in this inner ring of high priorities:

— Withdrawing to think, to plan and to organise in anticipation of major events
— Relaxing by reading a book, fishing, running, napping or watching a television show
— Being with family or friends
— Enjoying a hobby or pastime that removes my mind from coaching

You must identify activities which are meaningful to you and so develop your own personal recipe for successful time management. If you are intent on achieving success as a coach, one of your priorities must be to set and to achieve realistic seasonal goals. Let us examine some of the key elements this task involves.

SEASON PLAN

One of your most important coaching tasks is to develop a season plan, which includes everything you wish to coach in the coming season: for example, sport skills, rules, sportsmanship and strategies. The process of developing this plan is outlined in detail in *Coaching Young Athletes* (Martens, Christina, Harvey & Sharkey, 1981). The first step in preparing this plan is to establish your instructional goals. These goals need to be compatible with your coaching philosophy and the philosophy of the governing body of your sport.

Shown in Table 3.1 are two sets of realistic instructional goals. The first set is for a novice squash team of ten- to thirteen-year-olds, and the second for an advanced soccer team of thirteen- to fifteen-year-olds.

Instructional goals are general statements of what you hope your athletes will know or be able to do at the end of the season. Notice that the goals include much more than just techniques. Consideration is made of all areas contributing to the development of a complete athlete. Winning is not included as a goal because it is unrealistic to predict individual or team results with any accuracy.

TABLE 3.1

EXAMPLES OF INSTRUCTIONAL GOALS FOR TWO SPORTS

Novice Squash *(Ages 10-13)*	*Advanced Soccer* *(Ages 13-15)*
The squash players will be able to demonstrate:	The soccer players wil be able to demonstrate:

1. Mastery of the fundamental squash skills necessary to participate successfully in practices and matches at novice level.	1. Mastery of advanced individual soccer skills necessary to participate in games at this level.
2. Accurate and complete knowledge of basic rules of the sport.	2. Acquisition of the attacking and defending patterns of team play needed to participate successfully in games at this level.
3. Appropriate sportsmanship behaviours in practices and games.	3. Appropriate sportsmanship behaviours in practices and games.
4. Knowledge and application of the basic strategies needed to participate effectively in matches at the novice level.	4. Development of positive personal qualities in practices and games.

Using these goals for direction, coaches can organise plans for achievement. This involves the selection of skills as shown in Table 3.2, and the organisation of an instructional schedule as in Table 3.3.

Once the instruction of skills has been organised, the coach can develop a series of more specific sub-goals of expected knowledge or behaviour for each of the remaining instructional goals. For example, the squash coach who wanted his players to demonstrate 'appropriate sportsmanship behaviours in practices and games' might develop the list of specific behaviours shown in Table 3.4.

The weekly practice schedule should be based on the organisation of skill instruction. Other specific behaviours the coach wishes to emphasise—for example, sportsmanship behaviours—should be listed and referred to when planning for practice. Regularly reviewing these lists will enable coaches to select appropriate behaviours (rules or knowledge) to emphasise during practice sessions.

TABLE 3.2
INDIVIDUAL SKILLS

Drives
1. Forehand
2. Backhand

Counter to drives
1. Forehand volley
2. Backhand volley

Service
1. Lob

Counter to service
length return of service straight or
cross-court

Volley
1. Forehand
2. Backhand

Counter to volley
length and width forehand and
backhand drives

Boast
1. Forehand
2. Backhand

Counter to boast
straight length drives forehand and
backhand

Lob
1. Straight forehand
2. Straight backhand
3. Cross-court forehand
4. Cross-court backhand

Counter to lob
volley length forehand and backhand

Drop
1. Straight forehand
2. Straight backhand

Counter to drop
length drive or lob, straight or cross-
court, forehand and backhand

TABLE 3.3

PARTIAL INSTRUCTIONAL SCHEDULE FOR SQUASH GOAL 1

Skills	Week 1 Sat	Week 2 Sat	Week 3 Sat	Week 4 Sat	Time (in minutes) spent on each skill for a month	Total
Drive						
1. Forehand	T(5) P(20) (P5)			P(5)	35 minutes	
2. Backhand	T(5) P(20) P(5)			P(5)	35 minutes	70 minutes
Counter to drives						
1. Forehand volley		T(5) P(20) P(5)		P(5)	35 minutes	
2. Backhand volley		T(5) P(20) P(5)		P(5)	35 minutes	70 minutes
Service						
1. Lob			T(5) P(20)	T(5) P(15)	45 minutes	45 minutes
Counter to service						
length return straight or cross court			T(5) P(20)	T(5) P(15)	45 minutes	45 minutes

NOTE

T(5) = Teaching of the initial skill for the first time in 5 minutes

P(20) = Practise the skill for 20 minutes

The initial teaching time for a new skill is 5 minutes for each new skill. During the practice period there will also be coach contact time with the pupils to reinforce the skill.

TABLE 3.4
SPORTSMANSHIP BEHAVIOURS SELECTED TO ACHIEVE SQUASH GOAL 3

GOAL 3

The squash players will be able to demonstrate appropriate sportsmanship behaviours in practices and games.

SPORTSMANSHIP BEHAVIOURS

1. Demonstrates proper control of emotions.
2. Demonstrates use of appropriate language.
3. Is courteous to opponents, teammates, officials, coaches and parents.
4. Is humble in winning and gracious in defeat.
5. Respects opponent as a person in winning and losing.
6. Abides by the rules of squash.

PERFORMANCE GOALS

The goals you establish in your season plan must relate specifically to performance and not to results. Remember, you and your players have control only over performance goals, not over the game result. Coaches should never establish seasonal goals such as 'winning the championship' or 'getting to national finals.' These are unrealistic and almost certain to fail. You and your players will inevitably be disappointed, even though in many respects your season may have been tremendously successful.

Performance goals enable coaches and performers to see genuine improvements. Improvement is a sign of success and should be rewarded. Performers who fail to win competitions and yet improve their performances can feel proud of themselves, for they are successful. Perhaps you have already noticed how outstanding performers who fail to win Olympic medals or major competitions are sometimes labelled as failures. It is unfair to impose these unrealistic goals on them. Clearly, just to be selected for an Olympic team is a major success and deserves praise, not criticism. Coaches should help performers of all ages and abilities to set and to achieve realistic performance goals. These goals will increase motivation and maintain enthusiasm throughout the season.

SHARING GOALS

How coaches manage environments, not just individuals, was described in chapter 1. Does your organisation support your goals and share your direction and expectations? It is unwise to assume that you understand

the expectations of your chairman, administrator or director of coaching. Similarly, do not assume that they understand your expectations.

Arrange a meeting with the people involved in your organisation to find out what they expect from their coaches. Be sure to have a well-thought-out plan with you; it can be the best spokesman you have. Show them your plans, outline your philosophy and discuss any organisational changes you wish to make. It is much easier to build and to maintain a programme when you know exactly what you can and cannot do and when you know that you will have support whether or not you keep the trophy cases filled.

Successful coaches build realistic programmes slowly and carefully. They determine what progress will be possible over one or more seasons given the level of available support and talent. At this stage, they determine responsibilities and delegate tasks accordingly. These coaches then establish milestones for evaluating individual and team progress at different points throughout the season.

Detail management

Coaching is full of details regardless of the level of competition or the age of the participants. If you forget or neglect these details you may prevent progress or even ruin a coaching programme. To have time to coach, you must first learn to manage all the details that go with coaching. Some details only you can handle. Delegate details to others wherever possible.

SEASONAL DETAILS

To reach your goals, you must take the time to plan, and planning involves careful thought and foresight. Detail management demands the same kind of close attention. What are details? They are the tiny aspects of organisation so easy to overlook yet which can significantly affect the success of your coaching programme. For example, have you ever arrived at a locked sport facility that you expected to find open? Or perhaps your team finished a game in the middle of winter and you discovered that the showers were cold because no one had remembered to turn on the water heater. These 'minor' details can assume enormous proportions if you are not prepared.

PRESEASON PLANNING

A physical education lecturer and basketball coach of seventeen years recently told me, "I write the details down before the season begins. Two other people then check the list to make sure nothing has been forgotten." A number of other senior coaches reported taking the same comprehensive first steps in detail management. One coach in charge of a club swimming team kept a notebook containing specifics on how long trips to distant towns took, the amount of spending money swimmers should bring along and how many officials were needed at a meeting. Similar records were kept by the coach of a junior rugby team. In a four-page handout, he told parents when practices would be held, what players should wear to games, which parents should bring drinks and when lifts were needed for away games. These coaches have discovered that once the details of a season are in place, it is much easier to assign specific responsibilities.

Before the season begins, you should meet your assistant coaches, your performers and their parents to discuss organisation for the forthcoming season. This is the time to discuss your coaching philosophy and expectations. Misunderstandings between parents and coaches are a frequent cause of conflict. To remind you of many of the pre-season details which need consideration, a sample pre-season planning checklist is shown.

PRE-SEASON PLANNING CHECKLIST

Know the structure and operation of your governing body
Establish your philosophy and style of coaching
Prepare an instructional outline and schedule for the season
Plan competition entry dates
Arrange transport for the performers
Plan for the selection of a team captain
Establish team rules and penalties with your team
Meet parents to talk about the coming season
Prepare and obtain instructional aids and materials
Schedule days and time of practices and games
Schedule officials for games
Arrange for the preparation of the playing area for practice sessions and games
Establish inclement weather practice procedures for outdoor sports
Arrange for protection of valuables during practice
Select assistant coaches and plan the season with them
Plan for a post-season evaluation of your programme
Arrange for your performers to have medical examinations
Plan a fitness programme
Know how accident expenses are covered
Know what to do in case of an accident
Plan proper safety procedures
Obtain personal liability insurance if you are not covered by your governing body

DELEGATING RESPONSIBILITIES

The players on one soccer team always had half-time drinks and cut-up oranges because their coach asked each player's parents to be responsible for drinks and oranges at one game. He also organised a telephone notification system which kept all players informed of changes; no parent had to make more than two telephone calls using his system. This voluntary coach was regional sales manager for a large oil company. "Effective managers get work done with the help of others," he commented. By assigning a few details to parents, he was able to concentrate on organising practices and coaching the soccer players.

Of course, some coaches do not have parents willing to help, much less assistants, managers or secretaries. The entire programme is theirs to manage. "You do what you can and don't let the details overwhelm what must be done to produce a successful programme," a voluntary swimming coach said. "Some records of individual performance just won't be kept,"

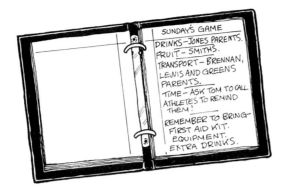

he went on to explain. "When your primary emphasis is on developing swimmers, the 'must' details are very clear. I tell my swimmers they are responsible for warm-up, equipment and for keeping individual time records. My job is limited to planning and running practices and preparing for 'meetings'."

If you coach on your own, staying within the inner ring of highest priority tasks is critical. Certain details such as arrangements for travel to a game, required entry forms and player medical records must be taken care of. These are the details absolutely necessary for programme operation. The rest you must put aside. Concentrate solely on your highest priorities.

COMPETITION DETAILS

Before a game or competition, there are always special details that need attention: the location may be new; different shoes, clothing or other equipment may be needed; the players may be introduced in a different way. These small matters can escalate if they are not given attention.

Competition should be given a little extra attention and difficulties or complications foreseen. "I call it problem anticipation," one judo coach reported. "Each meeting can produce special situations and associated problems which, by looking ahead, can be identified, anticipated and eliminated."

The time you devote to special preparation will vary depending upon the sport, the setting and the age of participants. Does the team know when and where the game is to be played? What colour jerseys will they wear? Who will bring the equipment and how will it get there? Although the details become more complex as the level of the sport increases, foreseeing details is crucial for all coaches. By taking care of the minor details before competition, you free yourself to concentrate solely on the performance itself.

Sometimes these minor details, if unattended to, can have serious consequences. For example, an assistant sprint coach on the 1972 U.S. Olympic Track and Field Team was responsible for ensuring that two sprinters made it to their qualifying heats. However, the coach believed the athletes had to be at the stadium at a later time than originally set. He did not bother to recheck such a crucial detail the day before the heats; as a result, the athletes arrived late and, after years of training, missed the opportunity to compete.

ELIMINATING DETAILS FROM PRACTICE

While managing important details will help you organise the season, eliminating unnecessary details can also improve the organisation and discipline of your training sessions. Establishing a routine is crucial when planning practices. Practices which follow a regular, well-known routine, especially in the period immediately preceding competition, are easier to administer and usually more successful. "My team knows when the season starts what training plan will be followed," a ski coach reported. "There is room for flexibility and change, but the basic routine remains the same."

Agreeing with that approach, a school athletics coach added that routine lets athletes know what will be expected of them each day. "They have certain drills to do, required conditioning and performance improvement targets to reach. I can't be all over the track supervising. This organisation allows me to concentrate attention on a few athletes and to know the rest are working." By creating a routine, you leave yourself time for spotting and eliminating problems, observing drills and helping individual athletes.

Setting limits

The graphic example of priority-setting shown on page 37 is your reminder to set limits. You must decide where each new activity belongs. Is it a first-, second- or third-priority activity? These decisions will not always be clear-cut, and sometimes you must take a chance. But the potential for task creep is enormous; avoiding Sarah's environment of panic and chaos is your best reason for setting limits.

Although establishing limits is theoretically simple, in practice you may initially find it difficult. Setting appropriate limits takes planning, and planning requires careful thought. It is easy to maintain old procedures simply from habit. Habit prevents us from questioning how we operate, even if we are operating poorly. Instead of taking the time to see if we have taken on too much or are over-accessible, we simply assume that we are operating as best we can. The result is a lack of improvement, efficiency or change.

The best way to set limits is to say no. Although Sarah and Frank operate very differently, they are alike in their unwillingness to say no. Sarah will not turn down unimportant tasks and Frank will not stop procrastinating. Contrast their approach with the following comments from several time-conscious coaches:

- "I won't take on speaking engagements at all during the season."
- "Encouraging new members to join the club is the only other major activity for the season besides training."
- "The responsibilities of assistant coaches are discussed and assigned well before the season begins. Each has specific duties which I know will be handled well."
- "My family knows they will see me less during the season. They aren't forgotten but preparation requires more time away from home. We talk about this sacrifice and they understand."
- "I find time to get away from the pressure to think, even relax, during the season—an absolute necessity two or three time a week."
- "I organise details before the season begins so that arrangements can be made early and most of the time by other people. These are never forgotten but don't get in the way of my major responsibilities."
- "I am less available to media and set up certain times when interviews will be arranged. I make some exceptions for the national media and distant reporters."

A single message emerges from all of these comments. Time is a scarce resource; you must use it intelligently and concentrate on a few critical goal-oriented activities. Think about your own coaching programme. What have you done to establish limits? Have you made clear to others what you will and will not be doing? Have you obtained their agreement to these limits? How effectively do you delegate tasks among your assistants? If your days are spent running, reacting and agreeing to do more, setting limits could improve this situation. Use the following list of reminders for setting limits to seasonal tasks:

REMINDERS FOR SETTING LIMITS

1. Allocate time to plan training and do not allow that time to be eroded, except for obvious emergencies.
2. Determine what you must do, and which tasks can be delegated to assistants, performers, parents and others involved in your sport.
3. Do not allow details to overwhelm you at the last minute: organise and delegate them before the season begins.
4. Focus attention and available time on helping young performers to develop; consider saying no to activities not directly related to that priority task.
5. Set aside time to relax, to withdraw and to evaluate the season.

Evaluating your programme

Coaches who are successful time managers find some time each week and often each day to look back and then ahead. They compare what has already been accomplished with the time and work remaining. These coaches review their performers' progress, examine individual and team performance in training and competition and consider any problems such as poor relationships between individuals and the team's general attitude. They check up on delegated tasks and evaluate the performance of assistant coaches, managers and other assistants. In the final step they identify any changes that need to be made—for example, shifting workloads or altering assignments. Although these coaches are not necessarily looking for trouble, they are trying to avoid the difficulties that often appear when one becomes too complacent or lost in details.

Evaluating involves taking a step back from each day's busy routine. "In my mind, I see the entire programme and the current season as they come together," a college rugby coach reported. He asked himself if his programme was on the right track and found that by removing himself some distance from it, he could come up with an intelligent and accurate answer.

"I find a few moments after training to evaluate," one swimming coach commented. "That is a lull period after a very busy time. Before training, there is too much to do to think clearly." Another coach reported taking an hour or two off just to walk and to evaluate the programme and season. "That time is part relaxation and part planning," she said. "The more planning and evaluation I do, the more relaxed I am."

The size of your coaching programme will dictate how much monitoring and planning is required. Even if you are not a full-time coach, you should take some time to think through what you are doing. As several voluntary coaches have observed, "That is how we manage our professional lives. Why should coaching be any different?" Use the questions below to help evaluate the condition of your own coaching programme.

1. How are individual performers and the total programme progessing? Is the rate of progress compatible with pre-season goals?
2. Are any problems beginning to appear? Between performers? Between performers and coaches?
3. Do I need to do more in certain areas or should I delegate more to others?
4. What is the general team mood now? Does it need any 'perking up?'

Direction brings improvement

Let us consider how goals, plans, priorities and other direction-setting techniques could improve Sarah Steel's training programme. Sarah would start each day knowing what had to be done and could identify her day's priorities. In spite of interruptions, Sarah would stay with one task to completion. If assistants, friends or others asked for her help, she would be more likely to say no because of her sense of time and physical limitations. Her vulnerability to task creep would be reduced.

With her goal orientation supported by a plan, Sarah would be less likely to hop from task to task. She would become more willing to delegate responsibilities to others and be able to concentrate her attention on high-priority tasks. Also, she would take on less and would not feel so pressured by a constantly expanding workload. Then, in the time she has available, she could further her coaching objectives. Sarah

would be determined rather than compulsive. More importantly, Sarah would realise she can be in charge of her work and life and enjoy the satisfaction of her achievements. Her talents would be used to help gymnasts grow and improve. And as coach, her attitude would be infectious, enabling assistants, gymnasts and support staff to use their time intelligently, too.

If Frank Adams recognised the need for goals and a plan, he might also appreciate that achievements are more likely with consistent effort, rather than last minute panic. Frank claims he does his best work under pressure and tries to avoid planning in advance. This contradicts an old and proven adage: "By failing to plan, you plan to fail." Research has shown that every hour spent in planning may save three hours in execution.

A better approach would be to use the full week rather than the last two days of the week to prepare his team for a forthcoming competition. A clear plan helps to set a measured pace. Frank might become more sensitive to others, instead of interrupting everyone early in the week and then later blaming them for the results of his own procrastination. A more consistent workload might also give Frank time to listen when he needs to listen and keep him from intruding on others' privacy.

Summary and recommendations

Good time management is a means to an end. To manage time effectively you must be clear in your own mind what you are attempting to achieve. Setting goals, priorities and limits will give you and your coaching programme a clear sense of direction which will increase the success of your coaching programme and prevent the creation of an ACORN environment. As you consider establishing direction for your coaching programme, keep the following recommendations in mind:

1. Goals should reflect the philosophy of *Athletes First, Winning Second*. Emphasise player development rather than game results.
2. Base your coaching programme on realistic goals; these should take into account reasonable expectations of what can and cannot be done.
3. Establish seasonal goals, then plan how to achieve them.
4. Assistant coaches, players and parents should know and understand the goals and the plan for the season.
5. Use the plan to help set limits and to determine what you and your assistants will not undertake during the season.
6. Before the season begins, focus your attention on detail management. Try to plan ahead and anticipate any organisational details which, if left unattended, could cause problems.
7. Evaluate yourself and your coaching programme to ensure both are staying within the limits you have established.

Uncertainty or indecision about what you are trying to achieve is the hallmark of an ineffective time manager. Establishing direction should be your first planning priority. In the next chapter you will learn how to sustain your attention on programme direction by controlling distractions present in the coaching environment.

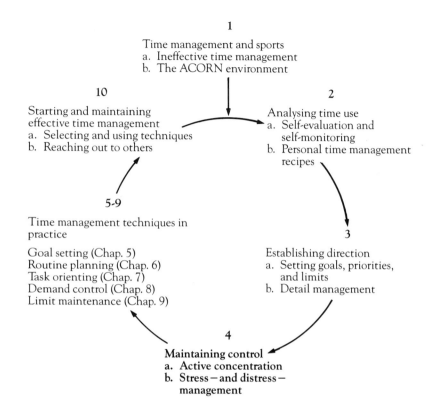

1

Time management and sports
a. Ineffective time management
b. The ACORN environment

10

Starting and maintaining
effective time management
a. Selecting and using techniques
b. Reaching out to others

2

Analysing time use
a. Self-evaluation and
self-monitoring
b. Personal time management
recipes

5-9

Time management techniques in
practice

Goal setting (Chap. 5)
Routine planning (Chap. 6)
Task orienting (Chap. 7)
Demand control (Chap. 8)
Limit maintenance (Chap. 9)

3

Establishing direction
a. Setting goals, priorities,
and limits
b. Detail management

4

Maintaining control
a. Active concentration
b. Stress – and distress –
management

Focusing on goals

Once you establish clear direction in your programme, you are on the path
to becoming a successful time manager. But, as you strive to reach your
goals, interruptions or pressures can prevent carefully organised plans
from being fulfilled. To manage time successfully, you must prepare
yourself to overcome these deterrents and to continue focusing clearly on
your goals. You need to retain control over your coaching environment. In
this chapter, you will learn about two techniques which can add control
to your day: active concentration and conscious distress management.

CONCENTRATION

Sarah and Frank do not have time, or make the time, to plan. They are
unable to step back and evaluate their programmes because they are so

frequently interrupted. Concentration is impossible under these conditions. Sarah creates this environment for herself and Frank creates it for others; thus, both have eliminated concentration as a useful time management tool.

Without the habit of self-induced concentration, Sarah and Frank give away their real time and rely instead on mythical time. When they do get down to finishing a project, they are under such external pressure that clear, careful thought becomes impossible. The results of this pressure are carelessly completed assignments and an ACORN environment. Pressured coaches, instead of concentrating on what really needs to be done, pressure those around them.

The experience of others who regularly give their work full commitment and intensity well before deadlines contradicts what Sarah, Frank and the people around them have to endure. They have discovered that minutes *can* be used intelligently and on high-priority work, that colleagues *can* be asked to wait or come back later and that doors *can* be closed. From these actions emerges a sense of purpose that translates into a determination to finish work quickly.

Like detail management, concentration becomes a useful time management tool when three changes take place:

1. Individuals such as Sarah develop a personal concentration routine and find ways to use it selectively each day.
2. Disruptors such as Frank become more sensitive to others' need for privacy.
3. People who work together establish traditions that allow for concentration through increased respect for the privacy of others.

Let us discuss the first change in behaviour — developing a concentration routine.

DEVELOPING A CONCENTRATION ROUTINE

Sarah is always telling her players to concentrate. "Watch the ball," she shouts on the practice field. "See the play in your head before you start," she advises during pre-match talks. "Focus on your goal" is another of her suggestions, for she is convinced that concentration is critical in mentally preparing for a successful performance. She knows from personal experience how effective this form of intensity can be. When she has time, Sarah often works with individual gymnasts who have difficulty concentrating. She will point out how, by increasing their attention, they will improve their performance.

The value of applying the same methods of concentration to her own tasks off the field has not occurred to Sarah. While she can motivate herself for competition or some other enjoyable activity, she finds it hard to get excited about paperwork. But completing these tasks is critical to the success of her training programme. Sarah and others battered by external and self-imposed interruptions need to blow a mental whistle and give concentration a chance. Coaches who try the following exercise often find that active and purposeful concentration contributes significantly to personal productivity.

A CONCENTRATION EXERCISE

Little time or effort is involved in making a concentration routine part of your day. It is easy to transfer the same attention you regularly devote to practice and competition to your programme administration if you follow these three sequential steps:

1. Recall
2. Experimentation
3. Regular application

RECALL

Recall requires thinking about what actually happens to you when concentrating. Consider activities other than sport; for example, reading a good book, painting, sewing, cooking, playing a musical instrument or singing can all stimulate heightened levels of attention. What activity absorbs your total concentration? Note the activity and how it makes you feel. Take a moment to consider when you concentrate most easily and most often. Here are some examples of activities and possible feelings:

Activity	Outcome (How you felt)
Reading	Totally involved
Painting	Relaxed
Playing an instrument	Able to hear the note in my mind before playing it

When an individual is focused on a single activity, researchers note the following:

— Activity receives full and complete attention; what was done before or might be coming next loses its importance.
— The environment is blocked out, eliminating any perceptions of noise or other distractions.
— The individual is self-confident and positive about doing well and tells him- or herself so.
— A mental picture of success appears, heightening determination and self-confidence.
— Separation from the environment occurs; the individual blends into the task, increasing the intensity and euphoria associated with its accomplishment.
— A 'flow', or attachment, develops between the individual and the activity; stopping becomes difficult.

Recalling the effects of concentration counters the battered mind. Using recall, Sarah, for example, could focus her attention on seeing one task to completion and be less controlled by what remains to be done.

EXPERIMENTATION

Experimentation occurs when recall stimulates enthusiasm about the usefulness of concentration for boosting individual productivity. Everyone is a little unique. People concentrate better on different tasks at certain times and in special places. To determine what combination of these three factors works best for you, do the following:

1. Identify two or three relatively short tasks you now do well. Routine but not boring activities are best. Sarah, for example, might fill out competition entry forms or compose letters to new players. She does these well when she has time.
2. Pick one or two periods during the day when your energy is high and interruptions are less likely; for example, early in the day either at home or the office, or just as most people leave for lunch. ·

3. Determine at least two locations, one at work and another at home,
    where you may be able to complete tasks with fewer disturbances.

'LOCKING IN' ON AN ACTIVITY

Try the following five-step process. It will help you to 'lock in' on
completing one activity at a time. With practice, your concentration
skills will improve greatly regardless of the attractiveness of the activity.
Before you begin, first identify a specific time, place and task. These
elements will enhance concentration. You may find that you do not need
all the five steps to concentrate.

THE FIVE-STEP PROCESS FOR 'LOCKING IN'

Selection of task, time and place increases concentration. Once this is
done, you are ready for the five-step process that leads to 'locking in' on
one task irrespective of its appeal.

1. Develop a frame of mind. The frame is a message to yourself that
    clarifies the importance of concentrating on one task. It increases
    your motivation because it clarifies your purpose, reducing any
    tendency to procrastinate. Motivation increases as a purpose
    becomes clear. For example, imagine the pleasure of having
    unpleasant work completed and being able to relax afterwards.
2. Relax for a moment. A moment of relaxation helps to shut out the
    environment and to focus your mind on the one task to be
    completed.
3. Develop a mental picture. Imagine yourself actually doing the task.
    This enables you to see possible problems and helps you to 'visualise'
    the final product. It also helps focus your concentration on the
    single task.
4. Take a few deep breaths. Athletes do this before a competitive event.
    It helps them to focus completely on their immediate goal. It can
    also help you to realise your goals.
5. Establish 'flow' with a directing message. 'Flow' describes what
    happens when task and person blend together when a momentum is
    established. Talking to oneself helps create flow by heightening self-
    motivation and directing it to a specific task. For example, you could
    say, "I'm going to finish this training plan this morning," or "Before
    tonight, I'll write all the letters to new players."

Gradually, you will find yourself able to expand the number and
difficulty of tasks you are able to address. You may also discover that the

results of improved concentration motivate you to find even more uninterrupted time each day.

REGULAR APPLICATION

Dedicated concentrators report five daily benefits from developing a routine.

1. High-priority assignments are given single-minded attention. This requires closing doors, asking some visitors to come back later, and even finding hiding places away from the flow of traffic. Concentrators let potential interrupters know they need some momentary privacy.
2. Improved concentration results in less task hopping. "If interrupted in the middle of a letter, I ask a visitor to wait for a moment," a school administrator observed. "Finishing just one sentence helps me return to the unfinished letter once the visit is over." Other managers learn to put phone calls temporarily on hold. The request for "just one minute until I finish" increases productive use of minutes and makes interruptions seem less jarring as a result.
3. Less reliance on mythical time is the third benefit of concentration. 'Concentrators' see minutes as gifts of time that can be used to write a letter, to read an important notice or to review plans. With these minutes, concentrators accomplish a great deal. They are organised to take advantage of unexpected periods which become available. If a meeting begins late or an appointment ends early, the minutes can be used to good advantage.
4. Reduced concern over what remains to be done is the fourth benefit of the ability to concentrate. With the single-minded focus that concentration produces, concentrators are mentally doing one task at a time. Digressive thinking becomes less common because one task has a tenacious hold over their attention. Consequently, little time is spent brooding or worrying about remaining tasks.
5. Concentrators become better listeners. Sarah heard only about one-third of the conversation with her troubled gymnast. She was busy panicking over what she still had to do before training. If her routine had included active concentration, she would have done more in the morning. Then, in the afternoon, she would have been able to listen and perhaps offer good advice to her distressed gymnast.

Coaches like Sarah need to recognise the value of improving their concentration skills and to try to incorporate these skills into their daily routine. Coaches who see how much this ability to concentrate contributes to sporting performance should recognise its value in an office setting. The same intensity and internal motivation critical to success in competition can be used to complete many tasks in the office.

Using concentration seems like a commonsense solution to a productivity problem. Unfortunately, not everyone behaves as expected. For example, coaches like Frank are insensitive to the impact of their behaviour on others, behaviour that can only be changed with some honest prodding from others.

LEARNING TO BE SENSITIVE TO OTHERS' NEEDS FOR PRIVACY

"You, you're driving me crazy" is the opening line to an old romantic ballad. In it, a lovestruck suitor describes his mental distress and inability to function. Assistant coaches, swimmers, secretaries and a host of others would like to say the same thing to Frank. For various reasons, however, they do not and Frank goes on making concentration difficult if not impossible for others. His behaviour suggests that privacy rights do not exist.

The best way to make Frank aware of others' needs is to point out the impact of his behaviour. Diplomacy is a better approach than a general indictment of his behaviour. Below are some sample statements that can help to open others' eyes to a need for privacy:

- "Can you come back later? I'm having a hard time concentrating on this report."
- "I'm sorry but I don't have time to discuss a new idea now—details have to come first!"
- "Excuse me, but I have to have this work done by 10.00, and I don't have any time to talk now. Can I get back to you later on today?"
- "Sorry, I don't have time for a story now!"

When candour is possible, and it is in many public and private settings, 'honesty is the best policy'. Through its use, individuals like Frank Adams may begin to realise that privacy is necessary and should be respected.

Unfortunately, there is no guarantee that Frank or others in leadership positions will become more sensitive to the effect of their actions on others. Furthermore, your position in an organisation can certainly interfere with honesty. You may not be able to change such behaviour, either because some individuals are unaware of how their behaviour upsets other people, or because you are not in a position to be so open. Under these circumstances, you might suggest another concentration technique.

ESTABLISHING A CONCENTRATION TRADITION

Employees at Marriott, Delta Airlines and IBM have a 'quiet hour' two to three times a week when relative silence and privacy are to be observed. Although this hour cannot be strictly enforced all the time, it has become a tradition in these and other organisations. Employees at all levels report getting far more done because of that hour and also discover they have increased respect for time as a valuable and shared resource.

Major corporations are not alone in their respect for time. Smaller public organisations are recognising the need for concentration as a part of each day's routine. Local governments, social service agencies, school district offices and other organisations have introduced some new concentration traditions. Nothing elaborate is needed to create such a tradition. In fact, single words or phrases such as the following can remind people who work together that concentration is necessary:

- Whoa—a moment of thought that should precede dropping in on another person: is it appropriate now or can the visit be postponed or cancelled?
- In writing—a suggestion that a note may be better than a visit.
- Set times—for individuals who are in regular contact; they should stay in touch but at pre-arranged times each day except for

emergencies.

— Really necessary—for meetings. Before a meeting is set, its purpose must be clear: no purpose, no meeting.

Respect for each other and the need for privacy are the reasons why these reminders are effective. People in the same environment who want to do a good job have agreed to establish a few simple traditions that ensure some privacy.

Consider what a tradition of concentration and privacy could contribute to your training programme. In an environment where interruptions are the rule, capable people do not have time to think about and then effectively handle so-called 'minor' details. Unless you ask others to understand and to support your need for concentration, you will probably have little success in doing it yourself. Sarah, for example, will not experience much progress until she decides to close her door and to ask visitors to come back later. Then she must get agreement from those she works with to respect the meaning of a closed door.

With a privacy tradition that allows individuals to concentrate, Sarah and others would be in control of their environment instead of constantly struggling. Changing attitudes and establishing a new tradition will not be easy. However, given the consequences of the ACORN environment and the battered mind, the effort is certainly worthwhile. Performers who concentrate in practice and in competition tend to be more successful than those who do not. You can achieve the same success by improving your concentration off the field.

Stress

For many coaches, the attraction of a book on time management is the hope of discovering ways of eliminating stress caused by poor time management. Harmful stress is a result of the ACORN environment and the battered mind. The chaos, the pressure and the exhaustion stress produces can limit your ability to function. How stress can help as well as harm you will be discussed in this section. You will see how time pressures and work overload cause stress and how you can learn to deal with stress on a lifelong basis.

WHAT IS STRESS

Not all stress is harmful. How improved concentration contributes to daily accomplishment was explained in the previous section. According to University of Chicago psychologist Mihali Csikszentmihalyi, concentration is a form of self-induced and self-controlled stress called eustress. Eustress is a positive form of stress, whereas other forms are not: psychologists call these other forms distress. You can think of stress on a continuum made up of six stages that produce increasingly harmful consequences.

Stage 1 At Stage 1 is eustress, which involves a mild stress usually accompanied by feelings of great zest, acute perception and excessive nervous energy. Individuals at this stage find they have an ability to accomplish more work than usual. The pleasant feelings associated with eustress can make it addictive. But human energy is finite and too much of this concentration can exhaust energy reserves, leaving an individual vulnerable to the next stage where distress begins.

Stage 2   This is where the unpleasant effects of stress begin. Energy reserves no longer last through the day but diminish after lunch or early in the afternoon. Occasional disturbances of the bowel and stomach functions, along with heart flutters, can appear. Typical reactions also include tightness of muscles in the back and around the skull together with a feeling of being unable to relax.

Stage 3   Individuals at this stage have more pronounced fatigue as well as greater disturbances of bowel functions, stomach troubles and muscle tightening. Increased feelings of tenseness, sleep disturbances and feelings of faintness without fainting are present.

Stage 4   For individuals at Stage 4, each day seems difficult. Activities that formerly were pleasant, including conversations with friends, become trying. Sleep is disturbed, a fear that cannot be pinpointed is present and concentration is all but impossible.

Stage 5   This stage begins a profound deepening of the previous symptoms. Extreme fatigue, difficulty in managing all but fairly simple tasks, great disturbances of bowel and stomach functions and pervasive feelings of fear are common.

Stage 6   This stage lies at the extreme end of the stress continuum and can produce terrifying symptoms. Common ones include a pounding heart and panic caused by adrenalin reactions, gasping for breath, or uncontrolled trembling, shivering and sweating. Numbness or tingling sensations in the hands and feet often occur. Exhaustion sets in and even the simplest tasks seem to require too much energy.

Where each stage lies on the stress continuum is shown below. How fast and how far you move up the continuum depends upon your environment and upon your tolerance for stress. You have already seen how you can change your environment. The latter part of this chapter will discuss how you can increase your tolerance for stress. But first, how can you get stress to work for you?

EUSTRESS

All of us have experienced eustress at some time, generally when we needed to accomplish a great deal in a specific period of time. In these instances, we have mentally prepared ourselves to do our best.

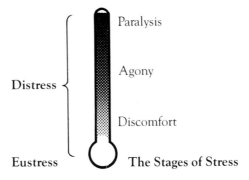

Distress {

Paralysis

Agony

Discomfort

Eustress   **The Stages of Stress**

Competitors are able to improve their performances by concentrating on single events for a short period of time. As good examples of eustress, the following performers have noted how concentration helps them to improve competitive performance:

— The diving champion talks to himself about the importance of each dive to build a necessary level of intensity before he climbs onto the diving board.
— The top tennis player focuses on each point in a tennis game to block out what happened previously in her match and to give all her attention to one serve or return shot.
— The centre forward of the soccer team concentrates on relaxing before a game so he can plan how to deal with the opposing team's full back.
— The cricketer relaxes before his turn at bat, thinks about the bowling he would like and then focuses his attention on scoring runs.

Of course, eustress is not restricted to competitors. Successful managers report how they focus their attention on a coming appointment or meeting. In addition to preparing written plans, they mentally review what will happen and how to do the best job possible on each occasion.

Executive secretaries, administrative assistants and others who coordinate major conferences, reports and projects use a similar kind of concentration, focusing on detail management. They think intensely about what must be done to handle each responsibility and write out important items they might forget.

Slowing down enough to think through each project, competition or practice produces a self-confidence that comes from knowing exactly where you are going and how you will get there. Self-confidence, together with the eustress that initiated it, can motivate you to continue to work efficiently, without distress. Unfortunately, too many individuals do not know how to make stress work for them. They cannot or will not control the pressure on them, they do not slow down and they do not take the time to relax. As a result, these individuals are less able to function effectively.

DISTRESS

Do you remember how fast Sarah moved from Stage 2 to Stage 4 on the stress continuum? On Monday, she was already near panic even before the lunchtime training session began. As the week progressed, stress continued to increase. Although Frank handled stress a little differently, his approach was just as ineffective. Frank's procrastination, last-minute pressure and unjustified blaming caused his assistants to move rapidly up the stress continuum.

Stress is a common phenomenon in sport. Coaches and performers are often under so much pressure to win: the pressure from parents, sponsoring agencies and fans can all serve to make sport exceedingly stressful. The inherent uncertainty of the outcome in sport, sometimes regardless of effort, only increases the pressure. Because sport is so naturally stressful, it is up to coaches to manage and to eliminate stress in those areas they can control. Research on stress emphasises the crucial role coaches play in keeping distress levels as low as possible. If coaches feel overly stressed, their exhaustion, negativism, tension and reduced self-confidence can influence the entire team.

Coaches and players inevitably experience some nervousness as they prepare for competition. While coaches, like players, use eustress to increase their self-confidence and emphasise excellent performance, coaches who assume unrealistic workloads are almost certain to experience distress.

Let us look at the example of a recently retired top soccer coach who took on too much in pursuit of success. During the season, he devoted himself completely to the team, engaging in dozens of activities without respite: he organised practices and prepared game plans, he constantly studied films of his and other teams and he had the coaching staff meet with him for long hours. Although the team was successful, the coach suffered increasing exhaustion. He resigned because of too much pressure caused by his unceasing drive for success.

Many other top coaches have left coaching for the same reason. Unable to control the pressures on them, capable individuals have been forced to make decisions which shortened their coaching careers but which probably lengthened their lives. You may have read about other successful coaches, men and women alike, in a whole range of sports, who also stopped coaching because of constant external and internal pressure to improve. For example:

— The local authority gymnastics coach who felt she couldn't say no to requests for assistance from colleagues. Her workload grew until she left for a less demanding position.
— The swimming coach at a major club, who could not get necessary assistance from parents, decided all the pressure had been placed on him, tired of it and resigned his position.
— The First Division soccer coach with a ten-year plus winning record who tired of fans expecting miracles each season and so asked to be relieved.

Because of pressure from a too heavy load or a win-at-all-costs attitude, these coaches pushed themselves to the point of physical and mental exhaustion. What these and other coaches like them did not realise is that their goals were unrealistic. Lacking realistic goals, they worked feverishly to achieve impossible ones. Instead of being pleased with reasonable individual and team progress, they were frustrated by their failures. In their rush to achieve, they forgot about organisation and time management. They forgot to plan, to set priorities, to concentrate, to give themselves a rest. Like Sarah, they spent all their time running, reacting and agreeing to do more. Their rush to achieve too much, in effect, ensured that they would achieve too little: they simply became too tired and too stressed to continue.

MANAGING DISTRESS

If you recognise yourself in these stories, then you need to learn how to handle and perhaps how to reduce stress either in yourself or in those with whom you work. Distress control is possible, just as eliminating the ACORN environment is possible. Whenever you feel under pressure, apply the following four-step process. It will help you reduce the negative consequences of stress:

1. Identify the causes of distress.
2. Identify possible solutions.
3. Emphasise the positive.
4. Respond rationally.

Identify the causes of distress   Identifying the causes of distress is an essential first step to managing it. Too often, we experience tension that if left to fester can begin to control us. Often, several things working together can produce unhealthy stress levels and make identification of a single source difficult. Listed below are eight common causes of distress to help with this identification process. Examples of typical coaching situations which can cause distress are also included.

Constant and unexpected changes
— "This revised competition entry procedure is effective immediately."
— "Beginning this week you will have to coach the junior squad instead."
— "The starting time has been changed; the team will have to leave three hours earlier."

Increasing demands on time
— "Please take on the fixture list as part of your regular workload."
— "From now on cross-country is your responsibility, as well as middle distance."
— "Please plan to attend all committee meetings."
— "Could you help to explain to these two new prospective coaches how they train and become qualified?"

Lack of guidance in making decisions or dealing with new tasks
— "Here is the problem, now go to it."
— "I'll be away for the next week and expect a full training report when I return."
— "There isn't time for explanation."
— "Everybody understand? Fine, can I expect the answers by noon?"

Relationships with others
— "All I ever hear about are her problems."
— "The chairman doesn't listen even when he claims to."
— "Can't those two ever be quiet?"
— "I suppose we have to work with Mr. 'No' now."

Repressed feelings and emotions
— "Nobody really listens to my ideas."
— "He shouldn't have been appointed athletic director."
— "Nobody understands the pressure I'm under."

Family-orientated difficulties
— "Our money runs out before the month does."
— "We don't communicate as much as we should."
— "The children just won't listen."

My work environment
— Too cramped.
— Too noisy.
— No privacy.
— Constant interruptions.

Time management problems
— Allowing priorities to remain unclear.
— Poor planning.
— Taking on too much.
— Procrastinating and creating pressure on self and others.
— Doing work others should.

You can make up your own lists and use them as a guide, or you may want to involve your co-workers in identifying causes of distress. Often, by openly discussing the causes of pressure you, as a group, can begin to identify specific ways to deal with these pressures.

Identify possible solutions   In many cases, difficulties can be minimised or eliminated through discussion. For example, if Sarah had discussed the pressure she felt by being constantly accessible, the others might have agreed to leave her alone at certain times. Instead, Sarah suffered in silence.

Unfortunately, some pressure-causing problems will not go away because changes or additional responsibilities may be a part of your job. One way to lessen the pressure of a change is to view it as a challenge. Although this does not eliminate the pressure, it may help reduce it as you prove to yourself each day that the challenge can be met.

Suppose a valued assistant becomes ill and cannot work for a week or more. You and others fill in, taking on some of the assistant's priority jobs. Some activities are put aside. This is a common challenge all of us face and usually handle quite well. We also deal with arrangements that break down, equipment which does not arrive on time, and weather that forces games or meetings to be cancelled. Instead of collapsing, we figure out rational ways to handle each situation.

You must use the same approach with other causes of distress. Instead of believing events run your life, assess what you can do to lessen their impact. With a colleague, develop realistic solutions to changes. If you had to leave three hours earlier for a competition, you would have to evaluate the situation and adapt your plans accordingly. Handling new tasks or reorganising old ones is no different. Every day we all cope with change, demands on our time and many other possible causes of distress. Recognising that we *have* the ability to cope means we are more likely to *use* this ability regularly and confidently.

By identifying causes and solutions, you are taking an important first step in managing the distress in your life. Just as setting goals can become a habit, so can dealing with the various pressures in your life. Even handling some temporary pressure is an important way of learning how to cope.

Keep in mind that sources of distress do not remain static, for the causes you identify this week or this month may be entirely different from those you experience in the future. In healthy organisations, managers take the lead in looking at causes of distress and undue pressure. They hold regular discussions in which the entire group can try to make the environment better for everyone. Logical ways to minimise pressure emerge from collective action. Once you have begun to identify the causes of stress and search for possible solutions, the next step is to emphasise your achievements.

Emphasise the positive Self-respect is an essential element in distress control. Your confidence erodes as you lose control and tasks not finished or errors made only seem to emphasise personal failure. You can avoid feelings of inadequacy by taking one or more of the following steps.

Be proud of yourself
At the end of each day, mentally list what you have accomplished (and make a written list for regular review). A 'to do' list can be checked and work done erased. One coach told me that throwing away his completed list at the end of each day makes him feel successful.

Recognise your physical and mental limits
Learn to stop when you need rest. Find time to slow down and do not push yourself to exhaustion level.

Select a hobby or pastime other than coaching
You can experience a sense of relief by woodworking, painting or cooking.

Hobbies or recreational activities provide a mental haven during busy times.

Make time each day to relax
Relaxation, not collapse, allows you to rebuild energy by slowing down. Unless relaxation becomes a part of your daily routine, it most likely will not take place.

Incorporate some form of exercise into your daily routine
Studies have shown that self-image improves as physical fitness increases.

Do not become pressured by people and events
The questionnaire on page 73 can help you evaluate the level of pressure you feel. Circle the number which most accurately represents your response to the question.

HOW PRESSURED ARE YOU?

1. Do minor problems and disappointments get under your skin and rile you more than they should?

1	2	3	4	5
Rarely		Sometimes		Often

2. Are you finding it hard to get along with people? Are people having trouble getting along with you?

1	2	3	4	5
Rarely		Sometimes		Often

3. Have you found that you are not getting much of a kick any more from the things you used to enjoy: for example, watching a rugby match, fishing or camping, seeing a film?

1	2	3	4	5
Rarely		Sometimes		Often

4. Do your anxieties haunt you? Are you unable to shut them out of your mind?

1	2	3	4	5
Rarely		Sometimes		Often

5. Are you now scared of people and situations that never used to bother you?

1	2	3	4	5
Rarely		Sometimes		Often

6. Have you noticed that you are becoming suspicious of people around you, even your friends?

1	2	3	4	5
Rarely		Sometimes		Often

7. Is there the feeling that you are being trapped?

1	2	3	4	5
Rarely		Sometimes		Often

8. Do you feel inadequate, just not good enough to cope?

1	2	3	4	5
Rarely		Sometimes		Often

The higher your total score, the more susceptible you are to harmful pressure. A dangerous total would be beyond thirty. Admitting you sometimes feel some level of tension is normal as long as you have methods to reduce the level.

Keeping up your confidence and fitness belong in your inner ring of highest priority activities. Remember, your attitude affects your entire programme; if you sink under pressure, it will too. The fourth step for reducing stress is to remain calm and attempt to think rationally.

Respond rationally You are given less than an hour to prepare an important statement. Three people with problems come in within minutes to see you, all wanting answers immediately. An assistant coach cannot make it to training. In situations like these, tension mounts quickly, and the pressure you feel can create some irrational feelings of inadequacy.

In your position, you are expected to act calmly and effectively, not with anger, panic or paralysis. Your first reaction to any sudden demand should be to take a few moments to think about the situation and how you will handle it. To accomplish this, do the following:

1. Temporarily reorder your priorities and put aside other work.
2. Clear an area so you can concentrate on just one task.
3. Develop a plan for preparing the statement or handling the work of the assistant coach.
4. Push yourself to complete the work using the concentration routine suggested earlier in this chapter.

These actions demonstrate that you are in control of a potentially disruptive situation. When the work is done, you can look back with pride on what your rational response produced.

I'm often asked about situations when three people want answers immediately. As several coaches have pointed out, each of us has but one mouth and one mind. Therefore, only one person can get an answer at a time; the other two will have to wait. You must determine which person takes precedence on the basis of the problem each presents. Once you have made this decision, you have established a plan of action and should give your total attention to the first question. Initially, you may not find this commitment easy; it will certainly test your concentration skills. However, you should recognise that it is the only realistic response and act with this conviction.

As you handle these and other situations, you will develop the skills of crisis sensitivity and crisis memory. These will help you to manage time and potential distress. Crisis sensitivity is simply a recognition that the unexpected is really an everyday occurrence. In our complex world, problems occur no matter how well-managed the person or organisation. If you are alert to the problems associated with planning a major competition, entering performers for championships or arranging a trip, you will be less surprised by unexpected events. You will also have time left to deal with problems because you will realise the need to set limits on your workload.

Coaches who use these techniques remember how similar problems were handled in the past. They may have prepared a list of details, phone numbers of people to call or logical alternatives. By relying on written records, these coaches are not handicapped by poor memories. Their written record is their crisis memory, allowing them to be more relaxed because they know that valuable information is readily available.

DISTRESS MANAGEMENT AS A LIFELONG ACTIVITY

Distress management is not something you do only when things get out of control. The ability to plan, to discuss and to react rationally comes from an inner calm and clarity. There are many ways to control distress on a regular basis; the following six have been suggested by the National Association for Mental Health (NAMH) as a starting point:

Ventilate Let off some of the steam by talking through problems with trusted individuals. They could be members of your immediate family, an old friend or a clergyman. Who you talk to is not important; what is important is that he or she has your trust and a willing ear. According to the NAMH, ventilating relieves the strain, puts worries in clearer light and can lead to rational and realistic solutions.

Move away   Take yourself physically away from the source of the pressure. Pressure builds in the most well-run organisations, causing you to tighten up. Even a momentary departure from the scene of action for a cup of coffee, a brisk walk or a chat can change your perspective. Time away gives you a chance to catch your breath and to regain the balance that pressure has a way of shaking.

Sweat away the anger Pressure usually starts working internally, causing headaches, heartburn or other mental and physical symptoms. Physical activity can help to release tension. To some extent, anger and frustration can be sweated out of the system. To his credit, Frank found time for a workout at mid-day. Given the intensity of her morning, Sarah should have considered a similar break.

Move on If you run into a block, do not let it become more significant by fussing or fretting over your inability to get past it. Put the project aside for a while and return later. NAMH research has shown that you will generally find renewed strength and a solution may emerge during the break. If you have had difficulty with an assignment in the morning, consider returning to it in the afternoon or try tackling only a very small piece of a problem.

Avoid perfection   Too many capable individuals are less effective because they constantly seek perfection. They expect a great deal of themselves and feel they have failed if they cannot immediately produce a perfect solution. Distress can be reduced if you orient yourself toward what you did accomplish rather than what you did not.

Give in   Do not stand your ground all of the time, even in those situations where you are completely certain of your position's merit. Yielding occasionally, according to the NAMH, reduces much strain on the nervous system and pays off in better all-round relations. Always fighting to win increases tension and makes opponents of colleagues.

In considering these six suggestions identify what works for you and mentally record these solutions for later use. By your example, you may encourage others to do the same.

Summary and recommendations

Excessive pressure can batter minds and lead to mental and physical exhaustion. Pressures can easily distract you from focusing on the direction you have established for your coaching programme. Improving your skills of concentration will help you control the pressures in your coaching environment. Coaches are naturally susceptible to the harmful effects of stress because of desires to win at all costs, setting unrealistic goals and failing to organise for consistent accomplishment. By building a healthy working environment, you and others in your sport will be able to accomplish the following:

1. Evaluate the total coaching programme to assess progress, spot problems and make necessary changes.
2. Find time to concentrate so that 'real' not 'mythical' time is used to finish work well before deadlines approach.
3. Impress on those who interrupt the impact of their behaviour on others.
4. Develop a concentration/privacy tradition that enables individuals to work alone as much as possible.
5. Remember that not all stress is harmful. Eustress can improve your performance and increase your concentration.
6. Avoid distress. As stress levels are permitted to intensify, the effect becomes increasingly unpleasant until individuals are unable to function.
7. Control distress by following the four-step process of (a) identifying the causes, (b) identifying possible solutions, (c) emphasising the positive and (d) responding rationally to potentially difficult situations.
8. Manage distress by using those techniques already described as well as ventilating, moving away from the source of pressure, exercising, moving on, avoiding perfection and giving in on occasions.
9. Recognise that distress management is a lifelong activity.

By establishing direction and maintaining control over their environment, all coaches can improve their time management. But, to become totally effective, some 'individualisation' must take place. The need to relate time management techniques to your own unique personality will be examined in **Part 2.**

Part Two:
Time Management Techniques in Practice

Creating a personal recipe for effective time management

A few years ago, a manager in a large government department showed what often happens when time management skills are pitted against personal habits. Six weeks after presenting a time management seminar at the department, I returned for a follow-up session. As various approaches were being reviewed, this manager related that none were working for her.

"None?" I asked with obvious embarrassment.

"Not the way you described," she responded. "They wouldn't work in my position so I made some changes. Now I have my own recipe!"

Her comments started a spirited discussion about personal time management recipes. One person in the group compared time management to the preparation of homemade chilli: fine touches make each person's version a little different.

There is no single 'right' way to manage time. A high degree of personalisation takes place in the use of specific time management techniques. Some individuals lean toward complex procedures like detailed schedules and extensive self and staff reminders, while others work best with only a quickly scrawled series of notes. Through a process of trial and error, each of us becomes committed to a few approaches that work best for us. We, in essence, create our own recipes for time management.

Everyone has a personal style of management. Even disorganisation represents a style. So, too, does waiting until the last minute to work feverishly under pressure. When individuals make improvements in time management, they complement and add to techniques already established. Consider these improvements as the bark around a tree. The bark surrounds and reinforces an already established core. Whatever new approaches you choose must fit around an organising core already in place; in other words, you must use time management techniques that fit your personality or you most likely will not use them at all.

Logically adding to what works

Bob, a local businessman and part-time tennis coach, asked me to help him improve his time management. He felt his lack of organisation was affecting his success in both business and coaching. Bob was extremely energetic and had many good ideas, but he tended to overload himself, hop from task to task and spend more time on details than priorities.

We found a few minutes to talk after he had a lesson with a young player named Richard. Bob explained how he was building on Richard's natural athletic and tennis ability. "His forehand is his best stroke, so I'm working on that first." Bob planned to work on Richard's serve next because this was another skill Richard had picked up quickly. Backhand, lobs, and net play would follow later to expand Richard's overall game. At every lesson, Bob reinforced what worked. Richard finished each lesson feeling he was a little stronger in one or two aspects of tennis play.

Bob understood the similarity between his approach to tennis instruction and mine to improving his time management. "But I can't see the same kind of results Richard does when he hits a winning shot," he admitted. "Those successes encourage him to go on, learn more and practice and remain excited about the game!"

Improving time management did not appear to have the same 'emotional' appeal to Bob. To capture Bob's motivation, I suggested a building-block approach based on three techniques he periodically used:

— A weekly plan which emphasised business goals, ordering supplies, scheduling part-time help at the tennis club, paying certain bills and analysing where the business could grow.
— Pre-lesson planning for every individual and group lesson.
— Occasional short periods alone in his office to do the work he had identified on his weekly plan—Bob rarely used this technique, preferring to leave his door open, and suffered constant interruptions.

I suggested he use these three techniques habitually rather than periodically for at least one month. To increase that likelihood, I encouraged Bob to write these three techniques on two 3" x 5" cards, placing them in prominent locations in his office and home.

Then we discussed building on the basis of these three strengths in the same way that he was teaching Richard to play tennis. His weekly plan could help him clarify goals by simply adding a couple of lines under the heading 'Goals for this Week'. This simple addition encouraged Bob to think about what he could become—a successful tennis coach/businessman.

Another modification built on his pre-lesson planning. An experienced tennis coach had once told Bob how he obtained all of his players by referral from satisfied players or parents. "With a busy teaching schedule, you can easily forget about individual player's needs and lose the personal touch," the coach told Bob, "and that personal touch plus your teaching ability is the motivation which keeps players coming and staying."

Improved planning was the solution for other problems Bob was experiencing; these included training new part-time help, planning club tournaments, organising special activities for junior members and publicising weekend Open Days to attract potential new members. In an earlier conversation, Bob had mentioned that when he organised a lesson, he visualised both the player and what he wanted that person to learn. "I concentrate on both, then identify what should be done," he said. The same approach was relevant to training a new employee or planning a club event. "Concentrate on what that person should know and how you can make it clear," I suggested. "In your mind's eye, visualise what the employee should be able to do."

It is important to remember that these suggestions were made gradually, as was Bob's work with Richard. Both had a chance to absorb and to try out a limited amount of new information and experience the pleasure of accomplishment.

Recently, Bob and I began to discuss his irregular use of time alone. The daily calendar on his desk is blank except for lessons and other planned club events. I suggested he pencil in 'time alone' on his calendar, making it a daily event. Bob is now in the process of doing this.

The key to Bob's success is the logical addition of modifications or expansions to what already works. He remains motivated because he can see the relationship between these alterations and the improvements in his programme, which include:

—   More time to plan major club events because he has trained his staff to handle work he used to do.
—   A slight but evident increase in new members.
—   Fewer times when popular items are out of stock.
—   A 'feeling' that he is more in control of what happens each day.

Bob feels that the steps he has taken to improve his time management have produced significant results. He continues to refine his organisational methods by trying out new techniques and by evaluating their effectiveness. You must do the same to develop your own personalised system of time management.

Time management techniques

Through research, five clusters of time management techniques have been identified: goal setting, routine planning, task orienting, demand control and limit maintenance. In practice, these techniques tend to be interrelated. No one uses skills from only one of these categories. Yet it is clear that successful time managers do have specific strengths concentrated in one or other of the technique areas. For personal reasons, you may find one of these clusters especially attractive and relevant for supplementing your existing organisational techniques.

Goal setting gives a clear sense of direction. It also provides well-defined criteria for measuring progress. The commitment to a clear direction and the existence of clear progress measures produce a desire for excellence. Goal-oriented individuals plan for the long term and are regularly thinking ahead. A sense of where they want to be is their trigger for activity. However, these individuals do not lose sight of the present and are constantly searching for new challenges.

Routine planning provides a structure or framework for getting work done. Before action begins, a plan must be made. Time is assigned to certain regular responsibilities. Special projects are analysed and time is allotted to them. In order for the routine to be effective, those with a planning orientation attempt to manage interruptions and control paperwork. Low-priority tasks are handled as quickly as possible. A person with these skills often finds that a routine is the motivator to begin work and to stay on track.

Task orienting helps develop ways to concentrate on one task at a time. Immediate job responsibilities take precedence over more interesting but less significant activities. The details of each task are not forgotten, and nothing is too small for attention. Individuals who are task oriented rarely make assumptions about details. With this emphasis comes a willingness to remove distractions from an office or to find a distraction-free environment. Pacing oneself to complete work on time and an ability to follow up with others are task-oriented skills. Rather than being motivated by a long-term goal, task-oriented individuals get their motivation from the task at hand.

Demand control means that high priorities get immediate attention. That attitude is part of a calm and deliberate reaction to events. Crisis control is very important to these individuals; some develop a memory of past difficulties so similar ones can be addressed more easily in the future. They separate legitimate demands on their time from those which are inappropriate. Individuals who must handle many demands will often make themselves less available because withdrawing regularly is important to them. Meetings, a form of demand, are reduced in length. Responding to the highest priorities first is the force behind this orientation.

Limit maintenance is guided by a desire to maintain a steady and manageable work output. Individuals in this group are careful not to push themselves beyond endurance levels. They establish a pace and try to keep to it. Delegation is important to them as is time for thought and self-renewal. Constant self-monitoring helps them to maintain an even pace. Effective and controlled communication plays a part in their style; staying in touch with others is part of this paced routine. The motivator and governor to people with this orientation is a pace that can be maintained.

The coaches you will meet in the next five chapters have developed their own time management recipes based principally on one of the five clusters of time management techniques. These coaches are described to show you how they selected specific techniques to supplement their existing skills and to help them control and direct their busy daily schedules. Try to notice how each coach has a reason for wanting to improve his or her use of time. Without motivation, it is difficult to make any substantial changes in our daily behaviour. Identifying goals and planning how to achieve them gives us the motivation to persevere when it might be easier to give up.

As you read, decide whether any of the techniques used by the five coaches could help you. In chapter 2 you were encouraged to develop reminder cards to focus your attention on the time management techniques you currently use. Since then, some new ideas may have inspired you to modify your original selection of techniques. Shown below is a revised version of the advice you were given earlier for constructing a personal recipe for successful time management. This list emphasises the ongoing nature of the organisational processes which will bring direction and control to your training programme.

— Write down techniques which already work on reminder index
   cards.
— Post them in visible locations and review them periodically.
— Select new techniques which you feel may improve your time use.
— Integrate only one or two new modifications at a time.
— Develop the habit of relating your successes to your reminder list.
— Review periodically and determine what really works.
— Add modifications to the reminder cards.

Remember, because you already have time management habits based
on your personality, you will be able to make only minor modifications to
your personal style, not substantial changes. You may add two, three,
possibly even four variations or expansions to what you currently do.
These additions can give you an important productivity boost and can
bring more control to each day.

5. Goals above all

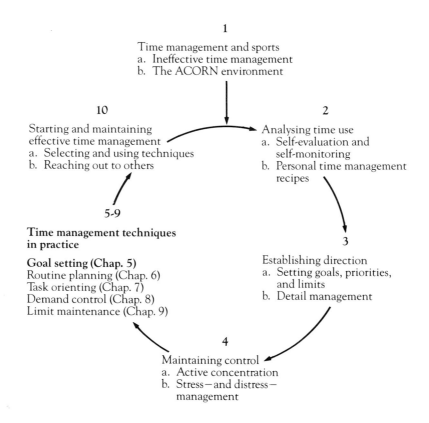

1

Time management and sports
a. Ineffective time management
b. The ACORN environment

10

Starting and maintaining
effective time management
a. Selecting and using techniques
b. Reaching out to others

2

Analysing time use
a. Self-evaluation and
   self-monitoring
b. Personal time management
   recipes

5-9

**Time management techniques
in practice**

Goal setting (Chap. 5)
Routine planning (Chap. 6)
Task orienting (Chap. 7)
Demand control (Chap. 8)
Limit maintenance (Chap. 9)

3

Establishing direction
a. Setting goals, priorities,
   and limits
b. Detail management

4

Maintaining control
a. Active concentration
b. Stress — and distress —
   management

Identifying goals: John Gibbs

John Gibbs knew he wanted to coach even when he was a schoolboy. "I loved to play, but my talent was just average," John admits. "What was really exciting to me were the opportunities to help others develop. Teaching younger kids just seemed natural, as well as being rewarding and enjoyable."

With that attitude, John became a coach during his time at university. Besides assisting the basketball and athletics coaches in university, he worked with the local clubs in the community. The more John coached, the more his enthusiasm grew. After graduating from university in chemistry, he obtained a teaching post in a secondary school where, alongside his main subject of science, he assisted with the physical education programme. John was involved in cross-country running, basketball and athletics. Other teachers assisted too, but none had quite his enthusiasm. John readily admitted he was a coach first and a science teacher second.

In addition to his work in school, John became chief middle distance coach to the local athletics club. "It meant some additional work, mainly administration, but I actually enjoyed that," he said. The more John coached, the more he knew this was his life's work. After five years working in the school and the club, he obtained a part-time appointment with his local authority. It was the next step in a carefully considered plan. 'Obtained' is an important word in John's vocabulary. He is a very determined and purpose-driven young man. All his life, John has made events happen rather than hope they will magically occur. In one sense, John is fortunate because he has always known that coaching was for him. Because of this, John was able to plan the steps in his coaching career. His next goal is to become a full-time coach working for his governing body or a local authority. "I enjoy making things work. The full-time coach's job is something to shoot for. The workload will include administration but I'd still want to be involved in practical coaching," John reasons. John is so aware of his goal he can easily identify milestones along the way. He uses these progress measures regularly and finds they increase his motivation to organise and to produce a successful programme.

Goal setting

Every day, John sets his sights on reaching some milestone on the way to that sought-after full-time coaching appointment. It was this determination which led him to apply for the part-time appointment with his local authority. Persistence paid off for John in a very real way: he identified an important objective and kept after it.

John thinks about the steps he must take to reach his goals. "There are many distractions and I want to stay away from most of them," he says. "Planning my life helps a great deal." John's sensitivity to distractions make him purposeful and he also knows when to stop and enjoy life. One of his goals is to have a balanced life that includes time for his family and for himself.

Planning his life through clearly defined goals is the foundation for John's unique time management system. He uses just a few techniques which put goals first, in harmony with his current responsibilities. His parents were goal oriented and John modelled his organisation on theirs. As a youngster, he was encouraged to set short-term goals in sports and studies. A teacher and his coach also advised him on the elements of successful time management, describing the techniques they valued. John listened and made some modifications to suit his personality. John's own time management system is based on goals he sets for himself and which he regularly reviews. These goals touch on what he wants to establish and to maintain in his personal and professional life.

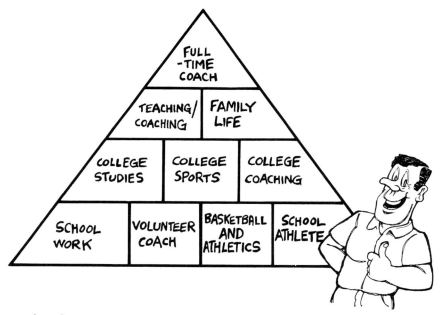

Personal goals: "I've watched too many coaches who are married to their sports with no time for family, relaxation and enjoyment," John points out. "That's not for me. My profession is important, but so is the rest of my life." Because of these beliefs, John examined some personal goals with his wife. Together, they determined the following:

— In what kind and size of community they wanted to live.
— In what part of the country (close to both of their parents and to the hill-walking they both love).
— The lifestyle both wanted and the income necessary to maintain it (his wife is now working part-time).
— The time they were willing to spend working on personal development, on community projects, socialising and relaxing.

John and his wife discussed their goals and made decisions based on their preferences. While both could easily be overwhelmed by activities and commitments, they take time to review their personal goals as part of each week's routine.

"It is easy to add more. Our friends and associates regularly ask us to chair a committee or help out in some way," John reports. "Our time is limited and there are certain essentials we both want. Saying no to requests beyond our limits is easier with these goals. We feel less guilt because the decision is related to our family plan and is not a hastily made choice which we would regret later."

Coaching goals: John defined his coaching goals to be consistent with his personal ones. He very carefully determined what was necessary to become a successful coach. He saw that he had to build a sound training programme and to help young people develop. With these two goals in mind, John was determined to do his best.

But John also had his eye on a position and setting where he would like to spend the majority of his coaching years. Through a long process of constant self-evaluation, John determined that a full-time coach appointment was best for him. Furthermore, of all the sports he had coached, he found middle distance the most enjoyable. He then discussed his decision with the people who knew him best and sought advice from past coaches on the directions he ought to pursue. They reinforced his decision to pursue a position coaching middle distance that also had administrative responsibilities.

Establishing a time scale

John also went a step further. Through conversations with his wife and close friends, he established a rough time scale for becoming a full-time coach. "Put the emphasis on rough," John adds. "But I do keep that goal in mind and take steps each day to reach it. Sometimes the steps are small, sometimes they're major."

John's yearly, six-month and three-month plans reveal his determination to advance. John believes that without them the pressure of his immediate responsibilities might eliminate any thoughts about the future. He feels opportunities spring from these plans and so relies on his own planning rather than luck.

John believes these plans give him time to grow and to become more capable. At the end of each year, he looks back on his coaching accomplishments and then identifies the next twelve months' targets. He honestly evaluates his coaching and administrative abilities at this time and determines where he needs to improve. He then determines which realistic activities will produce the changes he desires. Usually, those activities include a combination of organised reading, a few carefully selected courses and conversations with more experienced coaches. In addition, he is going to enrol on a coaching diploma course.

With the year charted, John can look ahead six months and then work back to what will happen in three-month blocks of time. "I have my eye on accomplishments over the short term," he says. "They boost my enthusiasm to continue." John gets even more specific, translating his goals into plans weekly. By doing this, he constantly reminds himself of progress to be made and of accomplishments already achieved. His progress evaluation is ongoing and he shares the result with his wife, associates and friends.

How much time does all this planning take? According to John, less than an hour each week. He has developed the habit of regularly looking back as the basis for projecting ahead. On a Friday afternoon, John looks back at the week's accomplishments and begins to sketch out his plan for the week to come. Then, on Monday morning, he takes about ten minutes to identify his major targets for the week.

John's weekly plan: John recognises that a variety of demands are made upon his limited time and is aware that he must fulfil his current responsibilities. "Building a training programme and working with young athletes is time-consuming and emotionally demanding," he emphasises. "It could drain away every hour in the day and leave me too exhausted for family and my lifetime ambitions. My weekly plan is the harness which keeps me from digressing too much. Some things will take me away from that plan, but I always come back to it."

Making and relying on that weekly plan is a habit with John. At the end of each week, he reviews what he has accomplished and then looks ahead to the next week. He identifies relatively few major responsibilities and tasks he must finish that week, as well as tasks he must at least start. This weekly plan also takes into account his personal growth targets and his family-related activities.

John shares his plan with the part-time assistant coach who is available three days a week. John and his wife share their weekly plans, being sure to cut back on their busy schedules for relaxation time. By sharing his weekly plans with the important people in his life, John can get feedback on anything he might have omitted, as well as keep everyone informed as to his intentions. "It takes very little time, reduces surprises for them and keeps me from forgetting," John says.

John's organisational system

One of John's organising techniques is to have different-coloured folders for major activities. He has found that this enables him to file his papers correctly and to find the right file when he needs it. He throws out those papers not fitting into his categories.

This filing system also involves another organising technique: evaluating papers of all kinds and deciding what he should keep. He throws out items for which he cannot find a use now or for which he cannot anticipate a use. John estimates that he immediately throws out at least 40% of all the letters, circulars and assorted announcements he gets. This leaves less to clutter his desk, office and mind.

"I find what I need more easily by organising paper each day instead of letting it pile up," John reports. The folders are an effective organising tool for him and are labelled as follows:

— Training schedules for individual athletes.
— Competition programmes.
— Athletes' personal records (medical history, injuries, etc.).
— Committee meetings or administration.
— Personal.
— Other.

He keeps these files on his desk and available for regular use with additional folders in a nearby cabinet. His filing system is a bit more elaborate. There are files for individual athletes and for some major responsibilities such as committees and reports he must prepare. But John has vowed to use only one filing cabinet because he believes more space usually leads to additional unnecessary clutter.

Plans and paperwork organisation which reinforce his clearly defined sense of direction are two important parts of his time management programme. But John also pays attention to a climate that increases his productivity. He knows certain athletes, students and colleagues have a rightful claim to some of his time: he realises that their habit of dropping by all the time could limit his ability to concentrate on one task at a time. Therefore, John looks for some simple ways to keep his mind from wandering.

Self-discipline

A few mental reminders help John keep on track. He uses three that a friend suggested and which he moulded to suit his style.

1. *Whoa* is his reminder to stop, think and ask. "What should I be doing right now?" This one word forces his attention back to his weekly plan and tends to emphasise the need to do the most important work first. When many people make demands simultaneously, John thinks of his reminder word to help him control frantic and purposeless activity.
2. *PF* stands for past and future and helps John to slow down and look back and then ahead. In the midst of busy and interruption-prone days, John plans for intelligent use of the limited amounts of time available to him. He organises the minutes between appointments and meetings for limited, but beneficial, accomplishments.
3. *Target* reminds John to ask himself, "Am I on target and dealing with high priorities first?" It helps John determine if a request is really important and enables him to control tempting distractions.

"These reminders slow me down and are my personal distress-control methods," John says. "They stop me from running off in too many directions."

These words keep John from climbing up the stress continuum. He has seen too many coaches allow events and other people to run their lives. Although John takes pride in being successful, he does not want to let his surroundings become unnecessarily frantic. These three words, along with his belief in his ability to manage each day, help John keep stress from reaching destructive levels.

These few techniques are John's personal recipe for time management. He is convinced they are enough to help him reach the goals he considers important. Although he has experimented with other methods, he finds he keeps returning to the same ones he has formed from habit.

You need not emulate John exactly, but you can examine his approach and learn from his experience and success. Selecting and adapting a recipe to suit your own style and personality is better than copying one you do not like.

The eight techniques John uses are listed below. Before you go on to chapter 6, take a minute to review these techniques and determine which, if any, you would like to consider as part of your own recipe.

JOHN GIBBS' RECIPE FOR SUCCESS

1. Establish yearly, six-month and three-month goals and monitor them regularly.
2. Develop a timetable for achieving certain major accomplishments and milestones to measure progress.
3. Ensure consistency between personal goals and coaching goals.
4. Plan for each week, emphasising high-priority work.
5. Communicate plans to key colleagues to avoid leaving out necessary activities and receive feedback.
6. Organise a filing system built on important activities.
7. Throw out irrelevant paper.
8. Use self-disciplining cues to slow down, to focus on the important and to control the stress level.

6. Planning for a complex life

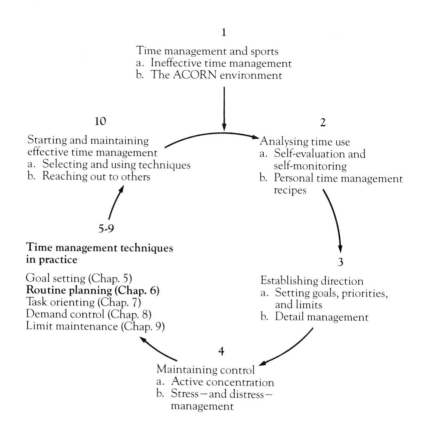

1

Time management and sports
a. Ineffective time management
b. The ACORN environment

10

Starting and maintaining
effective time management
a. Selecting and using techniques
b. Reaching out to others

2

Analysing time use
a. Self-evaluation and
self-monitoring
b. Personal time management
recipes

5-9

**Time management techniques
in practice**

Goal setting (Chap. 5)
Routine planning (Chap. 6)
Task orienting (Chap. 7)
Demand control (Chap. 8)
Limit maintenance (Chap. 9)

3

Establishing direction
a. Setting goals, priorities,
and limits
b. Detail management

4

Maintaining control
a. Active concentration
b. Stress — and distress —
management

Prioritising goals: Ann Davis

Ann Davis enjoys her job coaching girls' school netball, but that is only part of her busy and full life. "I'm what you would call a restless educator," she admits. "A lot of projects going on at the same time makes each day exciting." Her busy days begin very early. Ann, her husband and her children take care of their family responsibilities before leaving the house. The Davis family has a simple but effective plan that is the foundation for their morning and evening routine. Each of their duties is listed, including who prepares breakfast and cleans up afterwards. "I think the whole family is more comfortable with this plan," Ann believes. "Before we put it together, my husband and children tended to rely on me alone to keep the house in order."

Ann has been a planner all her life. "My parents always worked and were active in our community. Our family plan kept all five of us from going in too many directions at once and from forgetting our important responsibilities." Involvement also was part of Ann's life. "You get back as much as you put into life," her parents regularly advised. Thus, Ann found time to be on school committees and sports teams, in addition to maintaining a sound academic standard.

Living things have been a fascination for Ann since she was barely old enough to hold a frog. "Biology was naturally my best subject and teaching was a passion," she asserts. "It's wonderful watching pupils get excited about science." Her union is becoming another kind of passion. "Teachers have to act more independently," Ann believes. "Our union is a means, a legitimate means, to make our interests known." It is obvious from her comments that Ann feels deeply about the union. She has held an assortment of committee chairs and offices. "Never vice president or president," Ann maintains. "Then the union would become my whole life and there are too many other things that are important to me."

Netball is one of them, playing it with her sisters and on school and university teams. "I still practise with the players because the game is so much fun," she says. Her teams do win, but that seems secondary to the fun the players and Ann seem to be having in practice and at games. "Netball is enjoyable to all of us because we learn and improve," Ann adds. "We don't have the time or inclination to allow the players to goof around. They are all busy people and appreciate the discipline."

Family also is central to Ann's life. "Why have a family if you don't take time to be part of it," she reminds herself when she is overloaded with requests. "That is when my 'no' is very emphatic." As a mother, Ann does her share of volunteering in the children's school. Occasionally, she collects for a few charitable drives.

"I'm always conscious of overcommitment. My inclination is to say 'yes' or 'I'll get to it', which is really the same as 'yes'. Ever since a bout with exhaustion five years ago, I've learned to control that 'yes' tendency. Now I want to do just a few things well. What they are is pretty clear to me and to those in my life."

For Ann, those few things are family, teaching, coaching and the union. Ann has always sought excellence, put forth the extra effort needed to obtain it and, in fact, plans for it. In doing so, she uses a few time management techniques to support those plans.

Routine planning

Ann has the following three planning activities to bring organisation to each of her very busy and sometimes tense weeks:

1. Weekly plan.
2. Don't Forget list.
3. What Now list.

Like John Gibbs, Ann sketches out what she would like to accomplish each week in her four major responsibilities. "I try to identify what must be done that week or at least started," she says. "Procrastination has always been a problem for me. Keeping the important out front and visible, lessens the temptation to put things off. Although some work won't be due for a week or more, I go ahead and start it. I feel better when deadline pressure is reduced," she adds. On her weekly plan is a special column labelled 'Start,' under which two or three projects are listed. Each of these projects is broken into segments to encourage starting one piece in the time that becomes available.

Ann carries around her weekly plan in a loose-leaf binder that has sections for each of her classes and coaching work. The binder and her yearly calendar are with her all the time. "They reinforce each other and help me stay within realistic limits," she claims. For emphasis, she prepares another list to organise her busy life.

Ann's Don't Forget list is clipped to the top of her calendar. She makes it each morning just before breakfast, usually in consultation with her husband and children who also make similar lists and carry them around as reminders. With this list, she usually manages to complete necessary tasks, make important phone calls and attend necessary meetings. As a result, she has fewer crises caused by forgetfulness. Because Ann is constantly on the run, she keeps the list with her. It would be useless on her desk calendar because she spends so little time in the office. "A famous politician used a list like that," Ann reports. "We had a school visit to her office. We were awed by how much she did in a day. She mentioned the list. It seemed so logical then and is a habit now."

One more list helps Ann to concentrate and to slow down: her What Now list exerts a calming influence and minimises the pressure caused by a constant awareness of what remains to be done. "My days are really chopped up between classes, coaching and everything else," Ann says. "I'm an excitable person and what remains to be done could and sometimes does make me nervous."

When she had time, Ann used to waste it wondering what to do or she would decide she did not have enough time to attempt anything of value and instead would spend fifteen minutes or half an hour socialising. "It was half-hearted socialising," Ann recalls. "My attention was on all the work I had to do. But fifteen minutes never seemed enough time to do anything worthwhile."

A friend in the insurance business showed Ann a trick she'd learned from an experienced supervisor. "It's nothing more than slowing down to set some immediate priorities," this friend told Ann. "Instead of running around trying to figure out what to do or deciding to waste time, take a moment to plan." The idea of a moment to plan appealed to Ann. In her short periods of time, she thought about what she could accomplish during the day. From this emerged her What Now list. Depending on the amount of time available, she now works on parts of major assignments or completes routine tasks.

"My determination increases with those lists. Maybe I challenge myself to get more done. It is certainly easier to concentrate when I know my direction," she emphasises.

Learning to complete a task quickly

These short lists have made Ann aware of completion speed. "When I do a portion of a major task, the time it takes tells me about how long the rest will require," she asserts. "It's usually more than I anticipated. This warns me to start earlier on what's left to hold down last-minute deadline pressure." Her desire to hold down pressure also led to another technique for keeping the routine from overpowering her and her priorities. Ann learned the value of doing routine rapidly and now values this habit for its results.

When Ann began teaching, she was overwhelmed by the amount of paperwork. "How do you ever get through it all?" she asked a more experienced colleague. "I don't!" was the response. Ann found that her colleague ignored 70% of it and set aside the remaining 30% for review at some other time, usually when she was too tired to do anything important. Because her colleague believed that 70% didn't deserve her attention, she felt the chances of any problems arising from not reviewing it were slim. "If something is important enough to produce a follow-up letter or call, you will know a response is necessary," the teacher told Ann.

Ann was not entirely comfortable with that approach to paperwork. However, she did like the idea of doing routine and often low-priority work at one time. So, she developed rapid routines for doing routine work. When possible, Ann fills out forms at one time, records marks, makes phone calls and orders supplies. "I seem to do them more quickly as a group," she believes.

As she gained experience and confidence, Ann became more willing to tear up a request or throw out an informational item before reading it in depth. "The title tells me if it deserves attention or not," she says. Ann is equally concerned about reducing the impact that interruptions can have on each day. Again, her approach is an honest one.

Controlling interruptions

Ann learned how to control interruptions from another colleague. At first, she found it difficult to ask a pupil or player to come back later. "I told a colleague that I was a teacher and a coach, not to mention mother and union leader," she recalls. "Those are service roles. When people need me, I have to be available." That was an early rationalisation. Her comment, made in the staff room, was a response to a colleague who described all the ways he kept people away. Ann was irritated at his attitude and said so. After the exchange, a colleague she respected, and also a part-time coach, took Ann aside to point out a kernel of value in the 'avoider's' remarks.

This colleague advised Ann that although she should not shut people out, she should not let everyone have a claim on her time. She urged Ann to use some kind of control, perhaps by diplomatically asking a visitor the purpose of the visit. Ann's friend had found this directed the visitor directly to the problem.

Ann liked this teacher's honesty and the simplicity of the approaches she used. At a time management seminar for teachers, she had heard several gimmicks to control interruptions, including removing chairs near the desk, never sitting down when someone drops in, looking at the clock and lying about an impending meeting. These techniques struck Ann as dishonest and likely to lead to poor relationships. For Ann, honesty has worked. She now finds it easy to ask people to come back later, usually explaining why she cannot talk at that time. Although she takes time for necessary interruptions, she finds she now has more control over them.

Preventing procrastination

Another group of techniques keep Ann from relying on mythical time. Because she dislikes pressure, she has devised some mental cues which increase her willingness to start a task right away rather than to rationalise why it can be put off for another time.

Reminder phrases have become part of Ann's mental baggage; they are very similar to John Gibbs' mental-disciplining devices. She uses them whenever her tendencies to procrastinate emerge.

1. *Manageable units* tells Ann to break larger tasks into smaller ones that can be done in shorter periods of time.
2. *Opportunity for excellence* suggests that if Ann starts a task sooner, she will have a chance to review her work before it is due and make the final product that much better.
3. *Not worth a whimper* reminds Ann to get the seemingly unpleasant household chores done without thinking about them or complaining. "It takes more energy to complain than do them," she laughs.
4. *Effect on others* points out that procrastination affects friends, colleagues and pupils. When Ann's work is late, these people are under more pressure. Ann is especially aware that time is a collective resource. Because she dislikes pressure so much herself, she is sensitive to reducing it for others.

Reaching an organisational plateau

Ann's final time management technique is more of an attitude than an organising habit. Her technique is to pat herself on the back each day by reviewing what she has accomplished. That review shows Ann her unique time management recipe is working: she is completing what has to be done and maintaining the balance she needs.

"I'm as organised as I want to be," she points out. For Ann, planning, doing routine items fast, controlling interruptions and confronting procrastination are a means to a desired end; they are all she needs. With these few habits, Ann is able to meet her coaching, teaching, union and family responsibilities.

Do any of the techniques Ann uses appeal to you? Here is Ann Davis' recipe for successful time management.

Ann Davis' recipe for success

1. Identify a few central responsibilities and make a commitment to give them primary attention.
2. Plan for a week at a time and use that plan to identify a few projects that can be started early.
3. Prepare a reminder list of necessary details and keep the list with you at all times.
4. Plan to get the routine tasks out of the way in short periods of time.
5. Evaluate how long it takes to complete important projects so enough time can be allotted.
6. Develop routines to get the routine done fast and consider if any of it can be eliminated.
7. Control interruptions honestly by making others aware of your need for privacy.
8. Prevent procrastination with mental disciplining cues.
9. Pat yourself on the back each day by reviewing accomplishments.

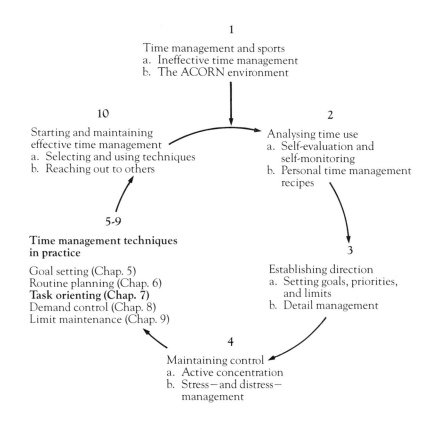

1

Time management and sports
a. Ineffective time management
b. The ACORN environment

10

Starting and maintaining
effective time management
a. Selecting and using techniques
b. Reaching out to others

2

Analysing time use
a. Self-evaluation and
   self-monitoring
b. Personal time management
   recipes

5-9

**Time management techniques
in practice**

Goal setting (Chap. 5)
Routine planning (Chap. 6)
Task orienting (Chap. 7)
Demand control (Chap. 8)
Limit maintenance (Chap. 9)

3

Establishing direction
a. Setting goals, priorities,
   and limits
b. Detail management

4

Maintaining control
a. Active concentration
b. Stress—and distress—
   management

Organising successfully: Ken Stephenson

"If I hadn't been born and raised in the Scottish Highlands, life really wouldn't have been worth living," Ken Stephenson often comments. It is his love of skiing that prompts this dramatic statement. Although Ken enjoys other sports and finds pleasure in the summers, he looks forward to the return of the ski season.

Ken admits he is addicted to skiing. "Not quite Olympic calibre," is how he honestly evaluates his abilities, but he has enough trophies and ribbons to demonstrate he is better than many. He even tried competition for one season after graduating from university. "That was enough; I went back to get an M.A. in Business Studies," Ken reports.

Master's in Business Studies in hand, Ken found a management position with a Scottish-based corporation. "Business was similar to summer—enjoyable, but not really engaging," Ken recalls. "I didn't look forward to each day with the same enthusiasm as skiing." So he took a risk and became a full-time director of a ski club. Ken now coaches many skiers, including some who compete in regional and national events. He has instructional programmes and an equipment shop to manage as well. For the present, Ken is the sole employee. If business increases, however, he may be able to hire additional staff. "I really have the best of two worlds, skiing and business," Ken says with enthusiasm. "Maybe the worst on bad days. Life is certainly exciting and very full."

Ken finds pleasure in helping young people develop and older ones overcome limited self-confidence. "I was surprised at my patience," he reports. "Encouraging others to learn is almost as much fun as competing."

Although Ken's club is only a few years old, its popularity has grown. Classes are full and clothing and equipment sales are steady. His coaching ability and business sense are a potent combination. Ken very much wants to see the club grow. His competitive and managerial experience have a decided effect on how he approaches what must be done to become successful and stay that way.

Ken was not always such a successful organiser. He did well enough at school and university to be admitted to a Master's Degree course. To help him get through the course, Ken met with a study group of other students, two of whom were 'super-organised.' They suggested a few time management techniques which would enable him to keep up with studies and still be able to ski.

Ken's personal recipe for time management emerged through experimentation and some difficult changes in his approach to life. "My old tendencies are still there," Ken admits. "I can still waste time on dozens of diversions, lose details in the process and fail to keep on top of all things. But each day I feel a little more disciplined and less likely to fritter away my energy." Ken was able to draw on certain disciplining skills competitive skiing had instilled. His desire to succeed is an important motivator now and he has found work truly enjoyable. Coaching brings him pleasure, as does an expanding club now beginning to make money. Time management is helping Ken achieve goals that produce regular satisfaction.

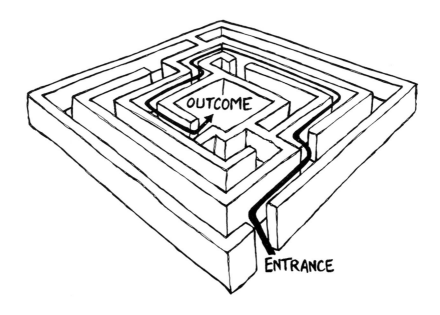

Task orienting

Concentrating on one task at a time is the foundation for Ken's approach to self-organisation. He generally works back from the outcome and due date to the beginning point of each major project. From that mental picture, Ken outlines all the activities or steps to be completed. He makes lists of what must be done each day and plots out the major tasks in his mind from start to finish.

"This method is a combination of how my coach told me to prepare for an event and the long-range planning that one of my Master's tutors described," Ken says. In both cases, the outcome becomes the motivator and what must be done along the way is clear from the start.

"There are some additional benefits to this mental planning," Ken reports. "Knowing the outcome desired and the steps to reach it encourages me to start sooner and to stay with an important task to completion, in spite of many interruptions." Instead of starting a new activity, Ken is likely to return to the original one and begin where he left off. This mental discipline reduces the impact of the interruptions which seem to occur every few minutes.

"You can't get ahead of yourself in skiing or business," he maintains. "With concentration, a downhill run or a budget will turn out well. Both need undivided attention from start to finish."

Controlling interruptions

"Enthusiasm can be dangerous," Ken believes. "I can get excited about all the opportunities and wind up going in several directions at one time. Sometimes it is just a case of daydreaming when I should be doing something more constructive. Whatever the reason, valuable time disappears and I wind up with too much left to do at the end of the day. Focusing on one task at a time helps me control the wandering my enthusiasm can produce." As an educational businessman, Ken is constantly interrupted. Multiple demands on his time are common. Because of this, it would be easy for him to put aside planning team practices, preparing for away competitions, stock-taking or paying bills in favour of answering interesting questions from a pupil or taking time for an unannounced rep's visit.

"I am more likely to postpone answering the question or taking time for the rep when I concentrate on finishing a task," Ken observes. "Obviously some interruptions cannot wait, but I find I listen better after finishing an important job."

Even when he is interrupted for an hour or more, Ken returns to a major assignment. The closer he gets to finishing, the more he is determined to complete the remaining steps. At this point, Ken 'locks into' his work and cannot stop even if he tries.

Preventing self-interruption

A combination of suggestions from a former coach and a fellow student showed Ken how he could stop interrupting himself.

The coach told Ken to commit himself to an excellent performance before starting, with a simple self-directing message: "Keep low all the way" was one such message. "It will build your determination," the coach advised. Within the limits of Ken's skiing ability, those messages did inspire better runs.

Now he uses a 'Before I stop' direction to himself as a way to prevent self-interruption. For example, he says to himself, "Before I stop, I'll have planned the team's next practice," or "Before I stop, I'll have finished the monthly order." This method encourages Ken to spend more time on finishing a single task.

What Ken learned from his fellow student was purely through observation. This student worked in a somewhat stark room, free of distractions. Her desk was not cluttered with extra paper and books and she kept what she needed within arm's reach to reduce the amount of time spent jumping up and down. Her room had adequate lighting and her chair was comfortable enough to prevent squirming but not so soft as to encourage napping.

Ken contrasted her businesslike setting with the chaos of his own study area. He had papers stacked everywhere, with 'get to's' mixed in with important material. When Ken started working, he thought about that student and contrasted her approach to his own disorganised, cluttered methods. He decided to make a few changes to his own style. He put his phone on his left side where it was easy to reach but not a distraction. He put his 'get to' pile on a bookshelf and skimmed all the material first. With this approach, Ken found that at least 50% of the paper could be tossed away immediately. He put major tasks in separate folders so that the paper and forms belonging together stayed that way. Finally, he arranged pictures and other clutter so they were not a constant presence and perpetual distractor.

Paper still accumulates in Ken's office, but his commitment to succeed makes his small office less of a storage area and more of a workplace. Furthermore, being able to find important papers faster is something he values. In a less cluttered office, he is able to keep himself self-directed, not self-interrupted.

Regular self-evaluation

To prevent himself from slipping back into old ways, Ken regularly self-evaluates. This helps emphasise the benefits time management is producing and also builds and maintains his motivation.

Once in the morning, once in mid-afternoon and just before the day ends, Ken slows down to look at his activities and accomplishments. "This is the time when I talk to myself; it's a one-man operation," he points out. Ken first identifies what he has done and looks at how self-organisation contributed to that success. Self-criticism comes next with the emphasis on logical and necessary improvements in planning and execution.

How and why did evaluation become a time management technique? Again his former coach and fellow students had an influence. The coach told him to assess his accomplishments and activities during and at the end of each practice. "We worked alone a great deal; our coach suggested that this would help us develop self-discipline," Ken said. "Without it, one flop could make us feel we'd never improve."

His fellow-students used self-evaluation to test how much of the assigned material they had mastered. "They called this brief review and self-examination a confidence booster," Ken adds. "Your motivation to go on usually increases when you can see the progress you've made." This technique keeps Ken's enthusiasm high and his discipline intact. "Not all the time," Ken admits, "but more than in the past. I wish someone had told me to self-evaluate about ten years ago when I was in college!"

Managing important details

"Those who don't study the past are cursed to repeat it": Ken had heard this proverb on many occasions. He learned the relevance of the principle during his Master's course. In one class, he was required to gather and to analyse details from past crises. The professors explained how several businesses had successfully used this data-gathering process to prevent future problems.

A visiting solicitor once explained that details were often essential for legal action. If an injured employee sued an employer, the manager in charge at the time of the incident would have to report what happened. Liability for negligence often depended on the manager's ability to remember the details.

Ken knew that negligence could mean lost money. He also realised that details captured for re-use would cut down the amount of time needed for planning and organising. When Ken started directing the club, he discovered how useful it was to collect names and phone numbers of key equipment suppliers, record transport costs and travel times to competition sites and keep a written record of other important details.

"In a one-person business, my time is an important company asset," Ken asserts. He keeps details on team and individual practices, competition organisation, and a number of business procedures he follows. He keeps them all in separate folders and habitually checks for guidance and for updating procedures. The files are a guide on which he relies each day.

"My memory is in writing," Ken emphasises. "No more looking around for old forms or calling friends who are more organised. I don't feel as pressured because I know where I can find important records quickly."

Setting and keeping deadlines

"I will never use 'as soon as possible' again," Ken says emphatically. "You can't run anything on the hope that you'll have work done when you need it. Deadlines and due dates have to be set."

In addition to erasing that phrase from his vocabulary, Ken now lists what he expects others to do and when. That regularly made and reviewed list contains names of team members, parents helping out with club teams, equipment suppliers and ski associations. Each day, Ken notes on a pad near his phone whom he needs to remind.

"Some people need to be pushed a little, others a lot," Ken points out. "But none of these calls takes very long and, most of the time, the work gets done on time. I just have to pick up the slack."

Specific dates and diplomatic reminders are essential to making this technique work. What's more, most of the people on his list expect Ken's reminders and appreciate them.

Ken is happy about his success in what he calls an educational business. "I enjoy making all the pieces come together," he says. "Teaching others to ski is almost as much fun as skiing." For Ken, organisation and time management are only a means to an end. It's the achievements—young people and adults skiing well, competitive teams and a business making money—that are so important to him.

Does Ken's recipe appeal to you? Listed below are the ingredients of Ken Stephenson's formula for successful time management.

KEN STEPHENSON'S RECIPE FOR SUCCESS

1. Focus on one task at a time.
2. Mentally establish successful outcomes for one task and work back to identify the details that lead there.
3. Organise a work area to be comfortable but distraction-free.
4. Do not self-interrupt; lock in with self-directing messages.
5. Self-monitor regularly to review accomplishments for an established period of time and use the review to encourage self-direction.
6. Capture important details in writing and develop reminder files with the details of regularly used procedures.
7. Set and keep deadlines for yourself and others, using reminders for individuals who tend to be late.

---

8. Sorting out the demands

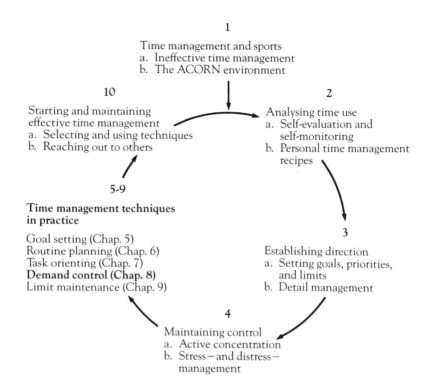

1

Time management and sports
a. Ineffective time management
b. The ACORN environment

10

Starting and maintaining
effective time management
a. Selecting and using techniques
b. Reaching out to others

2

Analysing time use
a. Self-evaluation and
self-monitoring
b. Personal time management
recipes

5-9

**Time management techniques
in practice**

Goal setting (Chap. 5)
Routine planning (Chap. 6)
Task orienting (Chap. 7)
Demand control (Chap. 8)
Limit maintenance (Chap. 9)

3

Establishing direction
a. Setting goals, priorities,
and limits
b. Detail management

4

Maintaining control
a. Active concentration
b. Stress—and distress—
management

Managing time and demands: Sandra MacKenzie

Sandra MacKenzie was greatly influenced early in life by a negative example—her father. All her adult life, she has thought about what a lack of priorities did to him. Now as a coach and teacher, Sandra tries to avoid the schedule which prematurely ended her father's life.

Jack MacKenzie was a well-meaning person who collapsed from a heart attack when Sandra was in the sixth form. As a factory foreman, he claimed his days were occupied by one crisis after another. "I watched the pressure kill him, even though we urged him to slow down," Sandra says sadly. "He had no routine. Even at home, Dad would drop everything if a friend called for help." Her father usually went to work early, skipped lunch and stayed late to catch up on unfinished paperwork. "He complained that helping so many other people made it virtually impossible for him to finish his own work during the day," Sandra recalls.

Nevertheless, he was always available and ready to help. Sometimes he would even volunteer for extra work, fearing no one else would step in to pick up the slack. " 'Can't you say no?' we used to ask him," Sandra remembers. "But even though he said he tried, he never knew how."

After her father's death, Sandra realised she had the same tendency never to say no. It just seemed natural always to volunteer and, because others knew this, she was constantly called on for assistance. Her father's death shocked her into acknowledging the consequences of such behaviour. She vowed to avoid the lifestyle which contributed to his early death. So Sandra began to look for people who, unlike her father, were able to manage time and the demands made on them.

Demand control

Sandra began to study her teachers and coaches and found that many had an ability to control demands. As both educators and people with family and personal responsibilities, they were very clear about what was and was not important. "I was really surprised at their determination to control demands on their time," Sandra recalls. The possibility of controlling demands without suffering negative consequences amazed her. She learned that people are more in charge of events in their lives than they often imagine.

The second time management habit Sandra noticed was that these same busy people also found time to get away, think, plan or just relax. "And nothing happened when they did," Sandra adds. "With just those two techniques, they controlled each day to a far greater extent than my father felt was possible. And look what they got done!" She went on to describe how these teachers and coaches handled a variety of responsibilities and had a life apart from their professional careers.

At college, Sandra began to experiment with controlling demands and finding time for herself. She backed off from all the commitments she used to make and tried to let her own needs influence her more than other people's agendas. Gradually, she became more comfortable with these two time management techniques. She chose English as her major subject and physical education as a subsidiary subject as well as working at her athletics; she also began to ignore many other minor distractions.

"I was always afraid of the consequences. I worried about what people would think of me if I said no to a request," Sandra reported. "Most didn't react negatively and there was less pressure on me."

Although Sandra found it relatively easy to use control at college, her new-found habits were sorely tried when she began coaching and teaching. The number of challenging activities seemed unlimited, and she was troubled about not doing enough for the pupils and athletes. Because Sandra coached two sports at school, cross-country/athletics and swimming, in addition to being in charge of the local women's athletics club and an English teacher, she had to develop high, middle and low priorities in each area of responsibility. Sandra is extremely capable but is saddled with a willingness to take on more than she can handle.

"But I'm on the alert," Sandra points out emphatically. Her father's death constantly reminds her to slow down her too-ready acceptance of just one more task. While she hasn't abandoned her willingness to help others entirely, Sandra also wants to enjoy life and to reduce the pressure that unrelenting demands can put upon her. Time management will help her reach these goals. Sandra's unique programme centres on controlling demands and finding time to pull back for thought, planning and relaxation.

Slowing down for success

"Continuing demand analysis" is at the centre of Sandra's time management programme. "It's not as fancy as it sounds," she hastens to point out. "All I do is analyse what I could do versus what I must do."

She learned much of her approach from a film show on a time management course. In the film, a busy and pressured executive was taught how to sort papers into stacks according to their level of

importance. This method involved pushing the low-priority material to last place or discarding it entirely.

Sandra adapted this method by putting low-priority work out of sight. "I use two drawers, one in my office at school and the other in my desk at home," she says. "I ask myself: Can this wait? If the answer is yes, in it goes!" As she is asking herself this question, she can rate the value of the paper altogether. In fact, Sandra finds that she throws out about 80% of it. That one step alone reduces the pressure on her. So far, she reports, there have been no repercussions from throwing out so much material.

Distinguishing the really urgent from the seemingly urgent

Blowing the whistle on the urgent is Sandra's second time managment technique. She learned this one from her college tutor. "What seems urgent to you, or more likely to someone else, will constantly try to displace what really counts. You could run in a dozen different directions at once and end up doing nothing!" she warned Sandra.

Every time something 'urgent' comes up, Sandra tells herself to 'wait a minute'. Those three words allow her to stop and look at what she is able to do and to decide if she should in fact do it. She gives herself a few moments to look at her primary responsibilities and to make a decision. Also, she uses phrases her father never did.

- "No, I'd like to help out but it just isn't possible."
- "You'll have to work it out yourself now; I just don't have time today."
- "Not this week, maybe next."

"Of course, I don't say no all the time," she emphasises. "But my time is limited and, if I weren't careful, my days, evening and weekends would be in others people's hands."

Sandra discovered that this method has positive consequences. She finds that people respect her time and she receives fewer silly requests. Consequently, she has more time for herself and for her athletes.

Finding time for personal needs

A coach Sandra respected once shared with her a valuable time management technique. This coach advised her that it is impossible to think on the run or when pulled in several directions at once. He emphasised that time for thinking, planning and relaxing was a crucial part of each day and told Sandra about the three periods each day he took out from his busy schedule:

- Before he left the house, he mentally visualised the day, jotted some reminder notes and prepared himself for a busy schedule.
- At midday during the season, he reviewed practice plans — off-season, he would relax with a swim, a walk on campus or lunch with friends.
- Early in the evening, he left at least thirty minutes free for relaxation or activities not related to coaching.

Because Sandra is not much of a morning person, she found that the first period did not work for her. But the other two were appealing and became a fixture in her daily routine. "They both are invaluable but for different reasons," Sandra reports. "An hour at lunchtime to think or get away is my control mechanism. In the run-up to competition, I spend it working on practices, fine-tuning the details." Other times, she uses the hour for herself. Once or twice a week, Sandra and a few teachers get away for lunch and she often finds a quiet spot just to read a book. Her evening slowdown is a seven-day-a-week, year-round habit. "I always find time for this. Sometimes I just sit. In good weather, I might go for a walk or a bike ride," Sandra says.

Getting to the point

Sandra also found that she was pressured by phone calls which seemed to go on for ever. When she saw an article in a popular magazine on how much time executives waste on the phone, she was immediately interested. "Half the time I lost interest or couldn't work out what the caller wanted," Sandra complained.

As a coach, Sandra has to get and give a great deal of information and most of the calls have to be sandwiched into a busy daily schedule. From the article, Sandra learned how to keep the calls to business matters and reduce the time each required. She particularly liked setting an agenda at the start of a call with direction-setting phrases such as:

— "I have four items to discuss with you."
— "Is this a good time for us to talk?"
— "Is there anything else we need to discuss now?"

She was amazed at how well-received direction setting was. "It was as if the people I called appreciated this organisation," Sandra commented. She found that keeping callers on track was more difficult, but by asking, "How can I help you?" Sandra was able to guide most callers to the point. "Most people didn't take offence and seemed pleased at being able to end a conversation quickly with results," she said.

Because Sandra found that direction setting was particularly successful for telephone calls, she began to use the same approach in meetings. "I want to find time for colleagues and especially pupils," she emphasises. "But some people seem to go on and on with no point in their conversation."

Slowly and carefully, Sandra introduced the same sort of phrases in meetings:

— "What do we need to discuss now?"
— "If I understand what you are suggesting . . ."
— "You would like me to do what?"
— "Is there anything else we need to discuss now?"

Although some of Sandra's colleagues joke about her efficiency, she notices that players who come to talk get to the point sooner. Team meetings, when they are held, move along purposefully. Sandra announces the agenda and stays with it. Again, she believes players and assistant coaches listen more.

Response efficiency

Sandra's final technique came from an interview she read in a local paper in which an executive discussed how she had cut down on the number of secretaries her firm needed. This executive found it was easier and less expensive simply to write or personally type a response on the bottom of the letters she received.

Sandra was a little nervous about trying the same technique but it appealed to her so she tried it anyway. Reactions were positive or at least non-commital. She found that she did paperwork faster by handwriting a response and that she could say what she needed to in a note, rather than a lengthy, typewritten letter. She also began making short telephone calls instead of writing a memo whenever possible.

These few techniques bring Sandra a level of control she values a great deal. They enable her to hold down demands, to feel less pressure and to contribute more as a coach and teacher. She still sometimes finds herself tempted to take on more and to treat every activity as a high priority but, by sorting out demands, controlling them and finding time for herself, Sandra is better able to distinguish important activities from those that intrude on her already pressured life. Here is Sandra MacKenzie's recipe for successful time management:

SANDRA MACKENZIE'S RECIPE FOR SUCCESS

1. Concentrate on controlling demands and finding time for yourself in the midst of busy routines.
2. Do not be afraid of controlling demands because of imagined consequences.
3. Sort out the low-priority work and put it aside for later or eliminate it entirely.
4. Put a hold on the seemingly urgent.
5. Find time for yourself and make it a regular part of each day's routine.
6. Encourage others to get to the point on the telephone and at meetings.
7. Respond with less formality and more speed.

---

9. Success from group effort

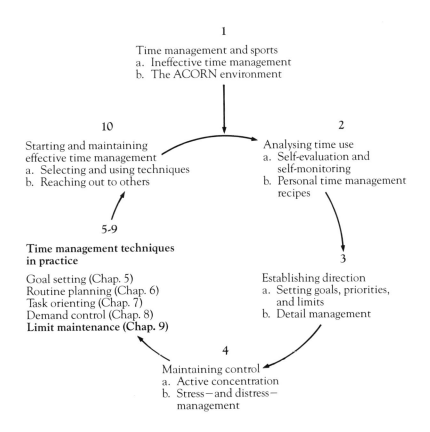

1

Time management and sports
a. Ineffective time management
b. The ACORN environment

2

Analysing time use
a. Self-evaluation and
   self-monitoring
b. Personal time management
   recipes

3

Establishing direction
a. Setting goals, priorities,
   and limits
b. Detail management

4

Maintaining control
a. Active concentration
b. Stress – and distress –
   management

5-9

**Time management techniques
in practice**

Goal setting (Chap. 5)
Routine planning (Chap. 6)
Task orienting (Chap. 7)
Demand control (Chap. 8)
Limit maintenance (Chap. 9)

10

Starting and maintaining
effective time management
a. Selecting and using techniques
b. Reaching out to others

Delegating responsibilities: Alfred Myers

Alfred Myers has to keep reminding parents he is a voluntary coach. "My family and business come first," Alf emphasises. "Coaching is great fun and I love working with the kids but it comes third on my list of priorities."

Alf is also honest about how much he will attempt as a voluntary soccer coach in a large and highly competitive local league. "How some of those others find the time is beyond me. Do they hold jobs during the season?" Alf wonders when he hears about the extensive and often complicated programmes of rival teams.

As the regional manager for an oil company, Alf has learned much about his own abilities and the consequences of attempting too much.

"Our company's success is the result of team effort, not of individuals working alone," Alf said. "That message is repeated again and again."

"When I began with the company, I tended to over-extend and eventually exhausted myself," Alf admits. Luckily, an experienced supervisor decided to help Alf out. He told Alf to keep a record of how he used his time for a week. The supervisor provided the forms and scheduled a meeting to review them. "At first, I was furious," Alf recalls. "With all the work I had to do, my boss was adding one more task of pretty dubious value."

Alf stayed angry for two days. But on the third day, he took a look at the forms and was stunned at what he saw. "My days were spent trying to do everything myself, which left me with no time to think and organise. I shut out the people available to assist me." The data Alf collected the rest of the week only reinforced his initial conclusions and he discovered that colleagues and his three assistants agreed with him.

Alf began to wonder why he had not realised this 'loner' tendency earlier. He discussed this with his supervisor who pointed out that as a student and project engineer Alf had been judged as an individual, not as part of a group. Until now, Alf had never had to depend on others.

Alf had to admit his boss was correct. He liked to work alone and was nervous about depending on other people. His parents had always said, "If you want a job done, do it yourself." But in an organisation where employees had to support each other to do the work well and on time, that approach was fast becoming impossible.

The need to depend on others and create a team spirit became the foundation for Alf's time management programme. His personal recipe is based on realistic dependence and the understanding that the load has to be spread out.

Delegating for success

Appropriate delegation is at the heart of Alf's time management activities. To prevent personal overloading, he thinks carefully about all the work that needs to be done, then asks himself a few questions to sort things out.

— Is this something only I can do?
— If not, to whom can the work be appropriately assigned?
— Is this person prepared now or does he or she need instruction?

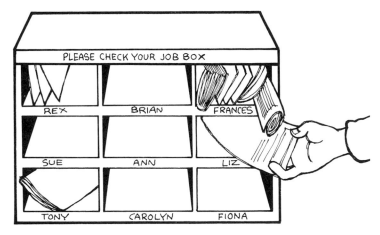

The second key part of Alf's time management efforts is ensuring that he has time to discuss what has to be done. Alf has learned that it is easier to motivate employees to complete an assignment when they know the job's importance and Alf's expectations. "I can't be too busy doing my own work or I won't have any time to discuss and explain the job," Alf now says.

Alf has adopted a few other techniques that reinforce those two basics. His programme has taken shape slowly with help from his supervisor and his colleagues' suggestions. In fact, his success at work made Alf feel comfortable about responding to an advertisement for voluntary soccer coaches.

Soccer had been Alf's sport from the age of eight through his student years. He played in school teams, local clubs and his university squad. In addition to playing, Alf had always wanted to coach.

"I just knew working with youngsters would be enjoyable," Alf says. "And it has been, with the kind of limits and self-management that prevents coaching from becoming a physical and mental drain."

All Alf has done is apply the time management programme which proved so successful in business to his work as an amateur coach. "Everyone associated with our team feels better staying inside some clear boundaries," Alf reports. "The kids know they will learn and enjoy the sport without crazy pressure to win from me."

Coaching continues to be fun for Alf because he sees the team as an organisation to be managed intelligently. He remains committed to doing a good job with assistance from others. "We are all voluntary and have many other responsibilities," Alf emphasises. "The team knows this and so do the parents. We all agree that setting limits is central to making this experience a pleasant one for everyone."

Providing clear expectations

At work, Alf knows how his performance will be judged. His superiors spell out their expectations annually, every six months, and also for shorter periods of time depending upon the project. When he realised that he needed a team to fulfil those expectations, delegating and instructing others became part of his routine.

As a voluntary coach, Alf received only general instructions from the league officials. He was asked to help the children learn more about soccer fundamentals, to build their self-confidence, to encourage sportsmanship and to emphasise the importance of playing as a team. "I thought about those requests, who the players would be, the amount of time we would be together and what we could realistically accomplish," Alf reports. "I made sure to identify my business and family responsibilities during the season, too."

Alf spelled out his realistic expectations at the beginning of the season. He wrote a letter to parents about what he hoped would happen, putting emphasis on learning, confidence building, sportsmanship and team spirit. He was careful to leave out any mention of winning. "The players have that so deeply drilled in I wanted to minimise it," Alf believes.

Alf emphasised he was a voluntary coach and would need assistance from parents if the team was to function. He asked for an assistant coach, a parent to organise transport to away games, another to look after equipment and a third to organise refreshments. The heart of Alf's team management was logical delegation. The assistant coach had specific and limited assignments. Other parents handled other details. Alf was careful

to limit what each was asked to do and to provide clear instructions. Getting messages across clearly the first time is a time management technique Alf uses on the job with great success. He finds it no less valuable as a voluntary coach, working with other volunteers.

"My goal is first time understanding," Alf reports. "Most people listen poorly, and unless I organise to compensate for that lack of attention, much of my time can be wasted."

His approach is simple and straightforward in all instructional situations:

— Announce what will be explained.
— Obtain a commitment from the listener to pay attention.
— Explain what must be done.
— Pause to allow time for questions.
— Encourage a trial or practice if applicable.
— Review or reinforce the main points of the explanation.

"Of course, the steps change depending upon the situation, the topic and the people involved," Alf adds. "But the goal of first time understanding remains; it is something I have to plan for." Alf claims he gets attention on most occasions—why?—because listeners sense he has thought out the instructions in advance and will not waste their time with unnecessary words.

Monitoring after delegating

Alf learned at work that an overcommitted manager has little or no time to monitor a job. By delegating, Alf is able to meet with individual employees, check on their progress and anticipate problems. As a voluntary coach with an assistant, Alf uses the same technique. He finds moments at practice and during games to instruct, to encourage and to correct players.

By taking a few minutes with each youngster, Alf believes he can emphasise soccer fundamentals and boost the player's self-confidence. This activity is an important part of his coaching, and something Alf enjoys a great deal. He finds those brief individual contacts motivate the youngsters, and he uses them to tell the players how much progress they are making.

This ability to find time for others has increased because Alf is willing to delegate, and he more willingly delegates because he finds time to instruct others. The two reinforce each other. Alf feels comfortable assigning work to others at work and on the team. He is also more comfortable taking time to plan because his workload is under control.

Regrouping mentally and physically

Alf used to feel guilty about taking time away from the job. He traced it to a work ethic instilled when he was very young that equated slowing down with laziness. His daily routine did not include time to think and to plan. It was his supervisor who emphasised the need for regular planning. He advised that lack of planning usually meant a lack of thinking.

Alf, however, was uncomfortable with the idea of planning. "It seemed so abstract to me," he recalls. "I couldn't attach any immediate outcome to it." At the company's annual managers' seminar, Alf heard a speaker discuss how to release creativity. During her presentation, she suggested using a pen and pad to jot down ideas. Alf liked this idea; it would give him something visible and concrete, some notes, maybe a plan of action. Alf began to use his pen and pad before meetings, practices or any event requiring thought and organisation. He gained so much from this practice that it became a habit.

At work, Alf scheduled some time every day to think, to jot down his ideas, in short, to mentally regroup. He would seek out a quiet location, the company library being his favourite. "There, I'm able to calm down, concentrate and get more done in a short time," Alf emphasises. "Thirty minutes in the library is equal to almost two hours in my office."

The thirty minutes of quiet preparation which he found so valuable at work also became a habit before each practice and game; the results were similarly positive. Those thirty minutes enable Alf to know exactly what will be done at each practice. At this time he prepares a brief game plan and makes a list of who will play, in what position and when substitutions will be made. Then he lets the assistant coaches and players know his plans at the start of each session. As a result, not only does his team know what to do but Alf finds he is able to concentrate more on the games and practices.

Organising paperwork

Alf's final organising technique involves collecting necessary information in the same place. At work and at home, he puts papers related to individual activities in separate folders. This method helps him find what he needs and reduces the amount of stored paper.

"If it doesn't fit into one of the files, out it goes," Alf says. "I keep only the paper I need."

Alf keeps all the papers related to coaching in one spot, and he keeps only what appears absolutely necessary for the team to function. He has three slim folders which he labels, 'Practices,' 'Games,' and 'Details.' If Alf cannot attend a practice or game, his filing system makes it easy for an assistant coach to find any necessary information quickly. Alf has organised practices so the team can continue in his absence.

Alf is much calmer with his personal time management programme in which success depends in part on working with others rather than alone. Alf remembers what life used to be like before he began delegating the workload. Just as he wants to enjoy and to succeed at work, he wants to enjoy coaching, not be depleted by it. He ensures that the responsibilities of running a team are shared evenly and that he spends his time coaching rather than chasing misplaced information.

Do any of the time management techniques used by Alf Myers have potential for you? The time management recipe summarised next should help you decide.

ALF MYERS' RECIPE FOR SUCCESS

1. Recognise the importance of delegating work.
2. Set limits based on realistic expectations and communicate them to the team, assistant coaches and parents.
3. Concentrate on getting messages across clearly the first time.
4. Monitor the team's activities and work with individual players.
5. Set aside periods to mentally regroup, to think and to plan.
6. Ensure that important papers can be located easily and quickly.

10. Starting and maintaining effective time management

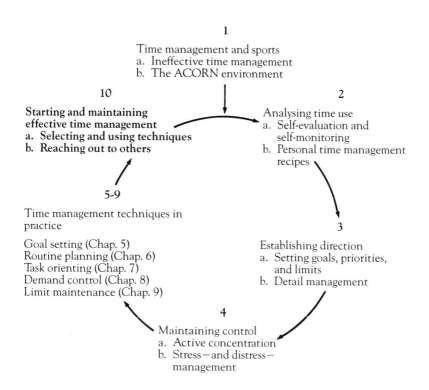

1

Time management and sports
a. Ineffective time management
b. The ACORN environment

10

**Starting and maintaining
effective time management
a. Selecting and using techniques
b. Reaching out to others**

2

Analysing time use
a. Self-evaluation and
   self-monitoring
b. Personal time management
   recipes

5-9

Time management techniques in
practice

Goal setting (Chap. 5)
Routine planning (Chap. 6)
Task orienting (Chap. 7)
Demand control (Chap. 8)
Limit maintenance (Chap. 9)

3

Establishing direction
a. Setting goals, priorities,
   and limits
b. Detail management

4

Maintaining control
a. Active concentration
b. Stress—and distress—
   management

Organising time effectively

"I want to be organised, but . . ."

It is so easy to make excuses for failure to manage time. Capable and dedicated coaches who use them belittle themselves by emphasising shortcomings rather than successes. On most days, these coaches successfully manage time, using techniques which have become habits for coaches like John Gibbs or Sandra MacKenzie.

Many coaches successfully manage time on calm days when they take the time to think, to plan and to act rationally, but on days like Sarah Steel's Monday or Frank Adams' Thursday, they exhibit mzungu behaviour—running around without any well-defined direction. These coaches treat the bad days as evidence that time management techniques are of no value to them.

Effective time managers use their time management habits to manage every day. By concentrating on achieving goals, they feel less pressure. Their lives are not free of the unexpected nor flawless, but they treat the periodic days when plans fall apart and priorities change as exceptions. Most of all, they believe in themselves and the value of a few logical methods to manage time.

This chapter will review the steps for starting an effective, personalised system of time management and offer suggestions for maintaining it. To prevent complacency, it is essential to review your skills periodically. As a busy coach, you must be alert to the same ACORN-creating conditions which undermined the programmes of Sarah Steel and Frank Adams.

Selecting appropriate techniques

No two people approach time management in exactly the same way. Thus, you must identify a few techniques which work best for you. Techniques can be divided into two groups: those which help focus on direction and those which help control pressure in work and non-work situations. The five coaches described in the last few chapters regularly used five to seven approaches, about evenly split between the two groups. Experimentation and help from parents, supervisors and friends led to their choice of methods. From hundreds of techniques, they selected a few which are listed below:

TIME MANAGEMENT TECHNIQUES FOR DIRECTION

1. Establishing yearly, six-month and three-month goals and monitoring them regularly.
2. Developing a time scale for certain major accomplishments and milestones to measure progress.
3. Ensuring consistency between personal goals and coaching goals.
4. Planning for each week with an emphasis on high priority work.
5. Sharing plans with colleagues; encouraging feedback and assistance.
6. Building a filing system based on key activities.
7. Preparing a reminder list of necessary details and keeping the list with you at all times.
8. Deciding to complete routine tasks quickly.
9. Assigning sufficient time to complete important projects before deadlines.
10. Segmenting large projects into smaller, more manageable units, using the short periods of time available during a busy day to work on these projects.
11. Setting and keeping deadlines for yourself and others using reminders for individuals who tend to be late.
12. Focusing on one task at a time by mentally establishing successful outcomes and working back to identify the details that lead there.
13. Sorting out the low-priority work and putting it aside for later or eliminating it altogether.
14. Recognising the importance of delegating work.
15. Setting limits based on realistic expectations and communicating them to the team, assistant coaches and parents.

TIME MANAGEMENT TECHNIQUES FOR CONTROL

1. Concentrating on controlling demands and finding time for yourself in the midst of busy daily routines.
2. Not being afraid of controlling those demands because of imagined consequences.
3. Controlling interruptions honestly by making others aware of your need for privacy.
4. Preventing procrastination with mental disciplining cues that encourage starting sooner.
5. Patting yourself on the back each day by reviewing accomplishments.
6. Organising your work area to be comfortable but distraction-free.
7. Avoiding self-interruptions by locking in with self-directing messages.
8. Writing important details and developing reminder files with the details for procedures regularly used.
9. Concentrating on getting messages across clearly the first time and encouraging others to get to the point on the telephone and at meetings.
10. Slowing down the seemingly 'urgent' requests by stopping to think before responding.
11. Finding time for yourself and making it a regular part of each day's routine.
12. Responding with less formality and more speed.
13. Setting aside periods to mentally regroup, to think and to plan.
14. Being sure that important papers can be located easily and quickly; throwing out irrelevant items.
15. Slowing down when you feel pressure and thinking about your priorities.

Use these lists and any other ideas you noted from previous chapters to develop your own unique programme for managing time. First, identify which techniques you already regularly use. Note why you use them. Do you develop written plans each week? Do you share them with everyone in your sport? A plan can guide your action and limit your activities. Do you try to get away to think and to plan for a period each day? With a list of what already works, you can begin to determine whether any additional techniques should be incorporated into your daily time management.

As you consider adding new techniques, keep in mind that many techniques require a behavioural change. Old behaviours do not change easily. Coaches who experience most success in improving their time management skills usually begin by selecting four to six techniques for an initial trial. They ask the following questions about each technique:

— Will the technique be immediately useful?
— Am I clear about how to use it?
— Will this technique require me to change my work habits a great deal?
— Will this technique fit into my organisation and be accepted by others on whom I depend?

Answering the first two questions should be easy. Most techniques you choose can be useful almost immediately. All that is required is some simple reorganisation. How to use the technique should also be clear. You may decide that maintaining a diary or a detailed daily planner is just too complicated and time-consuming.

The last two questions need more thought. Small habit changes which lead to improved time use are possible. Individuals who adopt new habits report slight modifications in time management. For example, a person may plan for a longer period of time, organise files differently, set aside more time for thinking or reduce the number or length of meetings. If change of habit requires too much trouble and too much thinking, success is less likely. Therefore, think about modest rather than major changes.

How the organisation and its members accept a new approach should be your next concern. I remember a manager who badly wanted to close his door to have more privacy. He neglected to think about the 'open door' tradition and why it was established. That tradition, the manager later found out to his embarrassment, was to encourage managers and staff to exchange ideas freely. Closing the door was an indication to others that he did not want to talk or to receive their opinions.

Privacy is pleasant and necessary. All individuals should enjoy it and respect the need of others to work alone. Unfortunately, there are some organisational traditions which make privacy difficult. By selecting an inappropriate technique, this manager embarrassed himself and probably felt less able to manage his time.

Selection is critical; choose slowly and carefully. Write down your initial choices and let them sit for a day or two. Ask your colleagues for their opinions of the choices. Some techniques will not affect others in the organisation: using lists or arranging files affect only the user. However, priority-setting or interruption-control methods definitely do have an impact, and you are well advised to obtain reactions before trying techniques which could prove embarrassing.

Using your new techniques

Once satisfied with your selection of time management techniques, you should make any necessary modifications to your index card reminders. Remember to leave these cards in visible places at home and work so you are constantly reminded of your goals.

Then, check the value of your techniques each day during the first two to three weeks of use by responding to the following questions:

— Do the techniques blend easily with your daily routine?
— As a result of using these techniques, do you feel more organised and productive?
— Are you starting to modify one or more of the techniques to suit your style and routine?
— Is it becoming easier and more natural each day to employ one or more of them?

With this evaluation, you can discard those techniques which seem more bothersome than helpful. As you review the value of your techniques, you should begin to notice an improvement in your ability to stay on task and to set limits to your daily activities. The habits you will develop include:

— Assessing whether you have set aside enough time to plan training, deciding when those times are and knowing where you can best work on this task.
— Setting aside sufficient time for detail management, for example, completing reports, planning trips and making calls. If you do not leave anything to chance, you will not find 'minor details' causing major difficulties.
— Reinforcing sound time management habits by seeing how effective they can be. If you look back on a well-organised week, you'll be more willing to focus on high priorities as you plan the next week.

Self-monitoring

Reviewing the value of your chosen time management techniques is a valuable first step in determining your progress. However, even after following all the advice and steps listed in this book, remember that it is very easy to slip back into old ways. Our fast-changing and pressure-filled environment often makes the immediate seem more crucial than the truly important. Regular self-monitoring will help you to refocus your attention on goals and alert you to the need for control.

Periodically, you should analyse your time use in depth. The time charts which were explained in chapter 2 can be used to analyse your daily schedule objectively. These charts will help you identify the source of any specific problems you are experiencing. This information, your own personal observations and comments you solicit from others in your programme will enable you to evaluate fully the success of your efforts to manage time better. Remember this progress review is an inner ring (high-priority) task. It only takes a few minutes and could well become a valued habit.

Believing in yourself

Self-confidence is essential for successful daily time management. If you believe days cannot be controlled, they will not be. Every example of poor self-organisation will be seen as proof that you cannot set and keep priorities or complete work according to a schedule. You may subconsciously expect failures and use the all-too-common, "See, what did I tell you!" statement when they occur. Your lack of confidence will affect other people who have to live with your belief that intelligent time use is not possible. You make it easy for them to give up too, perhaps leaving to find a position in a better managed programme.

As a coach, you tell your athletes they can succeed. Use the same approach with yourself and time management. Start out in the morning believing you are in charge. You can then plan the day's activities, write out a list or begin an important project. Remember your success, not your setbacks.

If you lack confidence, use a 'proof list' to remind yourself that you do manage time. Look back on what you have accomplished and identify the reasons for these achievements. A list helps boost self-confidence in pressured situations. A sample proof list is shown below. By identifying recent accomplishments and the organising approaches which made them possible, you will see that success is not due to luck—it depends on intelligent thought and action. To get started, think what you did to finish a recent major project or how you effectively handled routine work.

PROOF LIST

Accomplishment	Organisation
1. Finished training plans, arranged trip to county championships, obtained excellent accommodation	1. Closed door and worked alone for most of Monday evening
2. Turned in reports and expenses forms	2. Had file on past trips completed two weeks ahead of schedule
3. Completed letter to potential new club member	3. Grouped all routine work together
4. Identified problem team is experiencing with defence	4. Met with team captain on this topic alone; concentrated on that solution alone
5. Found time to develop tactics for next game	5. Delegated warm-up planning for first two practice sessions to team captain

In addition to proving you can manage time, this list will help pinpoint techniques you regularly use to manage time in more tranquil periods. With a sense of what can be done and strengthened self-confidence, you will be better able to build lasting habits that will lead to regular accomplishments and lower distress levels.

Staying in control

Contrast the organisation of Sarah Steel and Frank Adams and the five coaches who used time effectively. Coaches who are good time managers are intent on keeping pressure in check. They are aware of the distress potential in their lives and its negative effects. One of their goals is to control the pace of each day and the forces which can escalate tension levels. They use specific techniques such as stopping to plan action or finding time to relax regularly. Some are able to develop regular concentration routines.

In addition to achieving a blend of personal and professional goals, you must endeavour to stay in control. Remind yourself of this commitment every morning and evening by reviewing to what extent you were successful and why. By identifying the why, you know whether slowing down, finding a quiet place to work or asking visitors to come back later contributes to that control.

Everyone has good and bad days. Unexpected problems increase stress. Sometimes we allow ourselves to be irritated for less rational reasons—an imagined slight from a friend or even a traffic jam can threaten that

control. With a commitment to stay in control as much as possible, you begin each day and run your life with a positive "I can and I will" attitude. You are also more likely to know and to use specific techniques that produce desirable levels of control.

Through a sense of control, you increase the likelihood of achieving your personal and professional goals. All time management techniques are related to goals and control. Once you have established goals and are alert to staying in control, consider reaching out to others in your sport. As a well-organised leader, you are in a position to suggest how intelligent time use can benefit everyone.

Creating a sane non-ACORN environment

Time is a resource we share with other people. When it is seen as a resource and used intelligently, individuals can work together sanely and harmoniously. In organisations where time it abused, ACORN conditions cause disruption and bad feelings.

As a coach, you should work not only on improving your own time management but also on influencing how others organise and operate. As your personal recipe takes shape, share its components with others in your sport and explain your reasons for using certain techniques. This step tells them you are attempting to improve in ways that will be personally and organisationally beneficial.

Your honesty can begin other activities which can lead to both individual and group improvements in time management. The success of these steps depends upon your active involvement and leadership. When managers of organisations request time management seminars for their staff and do not attend themselves, a major problem that frequently emerges is manager disorganisation. Managers who are organised strive to create and maintain well-organised environments. They are concerned that others should use time intelligently and do not assume rational time use will occur. These managers actively work with all employees to foster improved individual and group time management.

As your time use improves, you can begin to reach out in the following ways:

1. *Explain your objectives and philosophy to performers, parents, assistant coaches and support staff.* When they know what is expected of them, their willingness to cooperate with you will probably increase. In addition, as you define what is meant by success, an emphasis on just a few activities becomes more logical. Just as you set personal limits, you are encouraging them to do likewise. Through regular contact and discussion, you can clarify and re-define objectives. When objectives remain clear and individuals know their responsibilities, enthusiasm to complete tasks is increased.

2. *Help create conditions where concentration and its important benefits are more likely.* By reducing the frequency of dropping in on others or, more emphatically, encouraging assistants to close a door, you build an environment free of constant interruption. You may also want to try cancelling unimportant meetings or limiting their length to a productive hour. Through these and related actions, you will give others an opportunity to concentrate and to avoid ACORN tendencies.

    Discussing how group time can be employed more effectively may lead to traditions everyone values. "Leave me alone time," a thirty-minute period in which individuals are to work alone twice each day, is one method that is used in several public and private settings. Another is 'to-the-point' short meetings where the agenda is announced before discussion begins. Reports that are shorter rather than longer is another tradition emerging from group examination of how time should be spent profitably. As a final step, you can encourage performers to manage their time effectively.

3. *Encourage performers to manage time.* A time-sensitive coach will help performers use their time effectively. Set an excellent personal example and emphasise how organisation is important in achieving success. Then suggest appropriate time management techniques to performers, depending upon their age and your contact with them.

    Some coaches regularly discuss goals with their performers. They mention the importance of these goals before the season and help individuals set their own targets. Then during the season, they emphasise setting limits on activities beyond studies and the sport itself.

    Other coaches encourage performers to improve study skills by setting aside specific times and places for these activities each day. A basketball coach reported that her players were required to study at certain times while the team was travelling. These examples are just a sample of the kinds of support you can provide for athletes.

    Much of your effort is aimed at helping performers to reach their potential. Better time use is just another way for that potential to be realised. Logical suggestions combined with regular reminders are two ways you can assist athletes to develop sound self-organising habits.

Conclusion

To be successful, you must believe in the value of your efforts. Effective management depends on your willingness to establish direction and to create conditions for achievement. A confident person will set goals and organise the time necessary each day to achieve them.

The second ingredient necessary for success is memory. Remember that we are all prone to allow ACORN conditions to develop. As a busy and energetic coach, you are likely to have many demands on your time. Remembering what can happen when time management is allowed to slip should help you emphasise the importance of sound habits.

Memory is also helpful on hectic and crisis-filled days when you begin to feel organising is just not possible. Treat those days as exceptions; if you allow ACORN tendencies to take hold, they can become the rule. Remembering that you are a sound time manager on most days will help you through the difficult ones. You will not be tempted to toss aside useful approaches because they were not appropriate on a few occasions.

Regular self-reinforcement is the third necessary ingredient. You should evaluate what a few sound time management habits produce. They will probably enable you to establish and reach your goals and to keep daily pressures under control.

Do not expect to change a great deal. Remember, you will have to mould any new ideas to your existing behaviours. By understanding how effectively you currently use your time, and perhaps adding a few carefully chosen new techniques, you will feel productive and in control. Apart from this, there is not much more you can or should do.

Index